MADE DEV(

C000219394

Chips Barber
and
David FitzGerald
with
Sally Barber

OBELISK PUBLICATIONS

ACKNOWLEDGEMENTS

We would like to thank the following 'extras' for their help, time and trouble in assisting us in putting this little production together: Anne Tirard, Myrtle Devenish, David 'Spud' Murphy, Eric Delderfield, Arthur Mann, Mr and Mrs Mason, Colin Jarvis (DNP), A T Bruce, Ken Green, Mrs T D Stokes, John Weeks, Christine Charlesworth, Joyce Becker, Tony Yelland, Lynda Spooner, John Earl, Mr Caymes, Jill Norrish, John Mann, Dave Knowlings, Jane Beeson, Jack Price, John Dean, Ern Vanton, Mrs King, Mrs Jerrott, George Pridmore, Mr and Mrs Finch, Mrs Coad, Mr Goddard, Barbara McBain, BBC Television Drama, Anthony Adams, Mr and Mrs Crooks, Sir Ian Amory, Clive Gunnell, and anyone else who recognises their contribution

'STILLS' ACKNOWLEDGEMENTS

Arthur Bladon for page 82
Bill Rogers for page 26, 27
Des Graham for page 56
· Jeff Bowden for 14
Brenda Schoolbraid for page 59
Spud Murphy for pages 40, 70, 72, 90, 91, 93
The Gable family for page 45
Paul Rendell for page 73
Terry at Oldway for page 28
The Postmaster at Drewsteignton for page 23
TSW for pages 4, 50, 51, 53
British Rail for page 81
Sidmouth Herald for pages 13, 15, 76, 77, 78
Dawlish Gazette for pages 19, 20
Julie Hodge, Exmouth Journal for pages 9, 10, 11, 16, 17
The Dartmouth Arms for page 38
Barry Hall for page 44
Devon Life for page 34
The Prospect Inn, Exeter, for pages 6, 8
The National Trust for pages 67, 68, 69
Ogilvie and Mather Advertising for page 55,
Jane Reynolds for the front cover
and Sally Barber for the back cover
All other pictures by Chips Barber

First published in 1988 by Obelisk Publications
2 Church Hill, Pinhoe, Exeter, Devon
Printed in Great Britain by Penwell Ltd, Parkwood, Callington, Cornwall

INTRODUCTION

Film makers have mastered the art of photographic deceit, so never believe what you see or where you see it. One of Michael Winner's first films was called *This is Belgium*. Unfortunately the budget was so low that the bulk of it was shot in East Grinstead! A film with its share of Ten Gallon Hats, called *Fate* and set 'deep in the heart of Texas', was in fact filmed in Sussex. Two rival companies both wanted to make films which featured the Berlin Wall. As the same wall could not be shared, one wall was built in Bradford for HTV whilst Granada constructed another wall only 8 miles away in Cheshire.

Here in Devon we have our own little deceptions, a landscape that the film makers have populated with plastic palm trees, mechanical crocodiles, electric penguins, chipboard castles and all manner of contrivances to recreate an authentic backcloth for a film. Devon has been used as the Mediterranean, Tropical Rain Forests, Liverpool in the last century, Monte Carlo, a distant planet, Dorset, Cornwall, Georgia, Scotland, Camelot, the Island of 'Cascara' in the West Indies, California and eighteenth century America to name but a few!

We have divided the book into three distinct sections, TV programmes, a short commercial break for adverts, and then films. In order to complete this book a vast amount of research has been done. We have talked to and written to many people, watched scores of films and programmes, often frame by frame, to produce this book. We know there are films and programmes we have missed and if you know of them, where were you when we were appealing for information? But there is only so much that can be fitted into a book of this size, we have picked out what we found to be the most interesting or amusing facts and incidents and hope you will agree and enjoy what you read.

TV Programmes Made in Devon

The Onedin Line

The Onedin Line must be one of the most successful and popular period series that the BBC has ever made. It was 'launched' in 1971, and such was its popularity that a further series was recorded and shown some five years later.

The setting for the story was Liverpool in 1860 and featured the exploits and adventures of Captain James Onedin of the Charlotte Rhodes, a three masted topsail schooner used for the shipment of various cargoes.

Cyril Abrahams was the creator of the series and was himself a vastly experienced sailor who drew on his extensive knowledge of maritime history in planning it. Vessels from ten countries were filmed in locations as diverse as the Azores and the Skaggerak. Unfortunately Liverpool of the 1860s could not be restored by the film makers so, using their own special form of magic, Exeter and Dartmouth became the principal locations. The tall warehouses on Exeter Quay were constructed in 1835 and therefore fitted the bill perfectly whilst at Dartmouth the antique charm of the lovely Bayard's Cove proved to be irresistible. Very little in the way of cosmetics were needed at Dartmouth to create an authentic backcloth, but a line of prop capstans were placed along the waterfront at Bayard's Cove. A young man arrived in his boat, tied it up, and then watched in dismay as the fake capstan broke off and his vessel sailed away without him!

A storm was needed for one scene which was filmed at Kingswear. This was shot on one of the finest days of high summer. Therefore a wind machine was brought down to the quayside along with the Kingswear Fire Brigade and their hoses. Curious visitors were literally roped in to help

◄ *John Thaw as Sir Francis Drake in "Drake's Venture"*

5

with the special effects. Several of them were given ropes to pull to make the vessel pitch and roll whilst the scene was shot.

Exeter Quay with its long, uninterrupted waterfront proved an excellent choice, being non tidal, particularly as in all film making there is often a lengthy time between takes and 'time and tide wait for no man'. Perhaps more than anything else the presence of Exeter's world famous Maritime Museum was another locational advantage with its expertise in sea faring matters and all its stores, rest rooms, boats and facilities also on hand to aid the making of *The Onedin Line*. Also members of the museum staff appeared as extras in the series in various roles which included coal hawkers, longshoremen, Arabs and layabouts.

The making of the first series was not all 'plain sailing' as for the two weeks of filming the sound recorders had to battle against the intense background noise generated whilst the new Exe Bridges, a few hundred yards upstream, were being constructed. The five year gap between series also posed a few problems. Obviously members of the cast had aged somewhat and some had gained some extra weight, and the relentless march of the motorway system in England was marked by an enormous viaduct straddling the Exe Marshes at Topsham. The significance of this was that the tall masted schooners, which used the Exeter Canal as the corridor up

Peter Gilmore (Captain James Onedin) and Anne Stallybrass on Exeter Quay

to Exeter Quay, all had to demast to get under the motorway bridge, a manoeuvre which proved to be an irksome and time consuming task. And, knowing how eagle-eyed viewers love to look out for 'boo-boos', you would have thought that the film crew would have been a little bit more careful about keeping the motorway bridge out of the background of a Victoria maritime England scene.

Harry M.S. Unsworth was a manager at Dartington Plant Hire when *The Onedin Line* was being shot. His firm provided the ideas and hardware for several scenes involving special effects. The Dart Estuary was used for the jungle scenes, the dense canopy of trees in high summer giving the right impression. Harry provided a floating pontoon to carry all the crew and equipment to shoot the scenes that appeared to be going up a typically tropical rain forest river. Strategically located, at various intervals, were imitation crocodiles or alligators which were controlled by extras who pulled strings to open or close their mouths or move their tails. The shoot went beautifully and those involved were invited to attend a special viewing the following day. When it was being watched someone spotted smoke, then a chimney and then the whole of a steam train plying its way along the Torbay and Dartmouth Railway to Kingswear. Many unrepeatable utterances followed.

Active volcanoes are in short supply in South Devon so the task of creating something which would reasonably resemble molten lava running down a mountain was a real challenge. A model mock-up would not suffice as a sea captain, an owner and two wenches had to be seen to scramble down the mountain side. At Totnes there was a tip near the hospital where Reeves, the timber merchant, used to dump tons of sawdust. The plan was to take a bulldozer and push ten tons of burning and smouldering sawdust down a slope whilst the actors descended across the effect in a diagonal direction. Everyone was ready and all were assembled complete with handkerchiefs up to the face to mask the overwhelming stench from household wastage dumped on the top. The sequence over, the actors thought they had a 'take' only to find that they were required to try again the following day. Unfortunately, when the retake was attempted, the wind changed direction and several actors were literally sick after inhaling the smouldering fumes. Happily everybody recovered and the final product was worthwhile.

The Prospect Inn on Exeter Quay featured heavily in the filming of *The Onedin Line* and its architecture and appearance must have had a considerable impact on the locations manager. Apart from the frequent glimpses of the outside of this popular inn there were many sequences filmed inside. Mrs Ruthven, daughter of Colonel Whitbread, managed to acquire several of the props used in making the series and close inspection of the walls will reveal quite a few Onedin souvenirs. Amongst them is a fine drawing of

The busy Victorian port of Liverpool—otherwise known as Exeter Quay

the making of the series by George Adamson, but you will have to search to find it.

The success of the series is reflected in the fact that it was sold to 40 countries from as far afield as Jamaica, Singapore, Australia and the Baltic countries. And it is interesting that it went down particularly well in sea faring countries like Sweden and Iceland. The human cast were in heavy demand all over the world to make personal appearances, but the Charlotte Rhodes rivalled Peter Gilmore in the popularity stakes! She was eventually sold to Holland, became unseaworthy and was the victim of a terrible fire and she will now only sail on in repeats.

Vanishing Army

This was a *Play for Today*, a series of plays that began in 1964 as *The Wednesday Play* but, for obvious reasons, was retitled when transmission was switched to Thursdays and then to Tuesdays.

This particular play was filmed at Heathfield Army Camp Honiton, which has since been pulled down and re-arranged as an industrial estate.

The play was televised in 1978 and featured the misfortunes of a Sergeant Major who was involved in two major battles, one in Northern Ireland and the other with his wife. Unfortunately the poor chap lost a leg in action and he spent much time in quiet contemplation about the times before his disability. Bill Paterson starred in this play and was ably supported by Brian Hall (who was 'Terry', the chef, in *Fawlty Towers*).

The Coombe House Hotel at Gittisham was used for a day, becoming the Officers' Mess. It seems that the 'army' of extras employed were, as usual, kept waiting around for considerable lengths of time between shots. Fortunately for them though, the Coombe House Hotel bar was open and many happy hours were spent there. However, several 'officers' did not behave like gentlemen and, having had far too much to drink, had to be dragged away for shooting – that is the shooting of the play, of course!

Big Jim and The Figaro Club

Even with such a distinctive title, this BBC comedy series set in the 1950s may not ring too many bells as it was shown on a late night spot and therefore was missed by the masses. This is a great shame as it was extremely funny in concept and in practice, with a similar theme to *Auf Wiedersehen Pet*.

A typically unconventional 'Figaro Club' creation sailing precariously out of Lympstone. Can you identify the seventh Dr Who?

The members of the 'Figaro Club' are Big Jim the Chippy (Norman Rossington), Chick the Brickie (David Beckett), Turps the Painter (Sylvester McCoy – the seventh television 'Dr Who'), Ned the Drainsman (Gordon Rollings) and Nimrod the tea boy (David John). The Clerk of the Works, often the 'villain' of the piece, was played brilliantly by Roland Curram.

The action was set around a building site where an over zealous and highly unpopular Clerk of the Works, Harold Perkins, made life unbearable for the workforce and they in turn got great satisfaction from extracting their revenge. For example, in one episode the tyrant got his come-uppance at a special ceremony to open a new drainage system and the workforce switched on all the taps, flushed all the toilets and emptied bathtubs of water to cause a massive flood which ensured that the proceedings were not exactly flushed with success. On another occasion they winched the foreman's highly prized car onto the roof of a hut and left it precariously perched atop it. The ultimate show-up for this much maligned man was a scene shot at Cockwood, an appropriate name, for he was set up and exposed in a very compromising position with an attractive young lady.

The Figaro Club on location at Lympstone Harbour

Exmouth, the golden resort of East Devon, was chosen for the bulk of the filming between August and November 1980. Sequences were shot at Elmfield Crescent, around the seafront, and at the Marley Gardens estate at Brixington on the outskirts of the town. It was here that many amusing scenes were shot including one where the site toilet was scheduled to be blown up as part of the action. The only person to be injured when this stunt was filmed was the safety officer!

On one day a scene was scheduled to be shot depicting a beer garden on a sunny day. Despite the fact that Exmouth has the driest rainfall figures for anywhere in Devon, it rained and the shoot was done extremely carefully making good use of umbrellas which were skilfully kept out of shot.

Another location used was Dawlish Warren, and Woodbury Common was the scene of another attempt to humble the foreman with mechanical rabbits wreaking havoc. Unlike many scenes shot on location, there were relatively few problems apart from removing modern television aerials and the prevention of any post 1950s cars appearing in view. There was a complaint from one person though – that the film crew was making too much noise whilst he was trying to watch television!

Roland Curram (Harold Perkins) being rowed out to his new boat by Norman Mitchell, the Commodore of Lympstone Sailing Club

One episode reached its culminating high spot at Lympstone. Harold Perkins, social climber, decides to take up sailing. Naturally the Figaro Club could not pass up such a golden opportunity to aggravate their boss so Chick the Brickie dons a wet suit and swims out into the Exe Estuary to drill a hole in the bottom of Perkins' boat. Meanwhile Perkins, who has dressed himself immaculately for the occasion looking every bit like the sea captain of the world's largest cruiser, starts to sink but goes down saluting. The rest of the Figaros are aboard a specially constructed raft and, like an unconventional RNLI, effect the rescue of poor, sodden Perkins.

The fun and games had to end but it did so on a merry note with a special award ceremony – the "DAFTA" awards. Gordon Rollings, who later did so many John Smith Yorkshire Bitter commercials (the one with the dancing dog and dangling wife from terraced house window), won an award for "The Study of Alcohol and its Effects on Location Filming" yet he was so taken with Exmouth that, after the filming ended, be brought his entire family down for an extra week's holiday, complete with dog, two cats, a budgie and a hamster!

And so it was that the Figaros left town not knowing whether their efforts would shoot them all to stardom or rocket them into obscurity. Some twelve miles of film were shot, and over four hundred costumes were used as well as a small army of local extras. The series created quite a sizeable following in a short time and was highly acclaimed for its freshness of approach. Plans for a second series were eventually shelved – what a shame!

Vanity Fair

This story of Becky Sharp satirizes the sentiments and pretensions of the upper classes in the first part of the nineteenth century. William Makepeace Thackeray's classic story has been much dramatized and although almost 150 years old, still makes a good yarn for sixteen Sunday winter evenings at about tea time.

Two days of filming were done in high class Sidmouth. Peat and sawdust covered the roads, false early Victorian lampposts were put in on street corners, all signs were masked and AA and RAC signs were boxed. Barrow boys sold baked potatoes and Vienna rolls, and fishmongers bawled out their wares on the pavements as baskets brimmed over with fish. Less picturesque were the huge bulldozers which were brought in to reduce the gradient of the beach so that old fashioned bathing machines

Behind the scenes in "Vanity Fair" at Sidmouth

Preparing Sidmouth Esplanade for filming "Vanity Fair"

Old fashioned bathing machines and changing tents on Sidmouth Beach

could be introduced. As can be seen from the photographs, everything combined to make a perfect set. Several other seaside resorts outside of Devon, including Lyme Regis, were used and the Battle of Waterloo was staged at Norwich!

The Children of Dynmouth

Simon Fox, John Bird, Avril Elgar, Peter Jones, Myrtle Devenish and Billy Burden were all in *The Children of Dynmouth* by William Trevor which perhaps should have been named "The Child of Dynmouth" as the plot centred on just one child, a disturbing character called Timothy Gedge. 'Dynmouth' in the film was Sidmouth in reality, just down the road from 'Dilmouth' the setting for an episode of Agatha Christie's "Miss Marple" series.

Under the front page headline "Fast Food Fury" the Sidmouth Herald covered a story which eventually ended in smiles for all concerned. An empty property, destined to become an estate agent's office, was rented for a short time and converted into a fish and chip shop for the play. A local town councillor was unaware that this was just a film set and somewhat indignantly informed the Sidmouth Town Council Planning Committee about it. Fortunately, when she was put in the picture, there was much amusement all round.

When film makers are around nothing you see should be believed. Outside this take-away they planted a very genuine looking telephone box, so genuine in fact that a great number of people tried in vain to make a call!

The 'fast food shop' which was so fast that it never opened—except for some fast filming

The story surrounded the antics of Timothy Gedge, a neglected teenager who manipulated his way into the annual local talent contest in the small town resort. His close surveillance of local people and their debatable behaviour is his blackmail ammunition to acquire the necessary props for his bizarre act. The 'vicar' was definitely not amused by his performance featuring one-time 'Brides in the Bath' murderer George Joseph Smith, for whom Timothy had developed an obsession.

When *Children of Dynmouth* hit the screens most people would have just regarded it as an unattractive play about a disagreeable character unless it

was their own town that was being associated with it. Most locals seemed to think it was bad for the image of a family resort and, having seen it, there was a general element of relief that Sidmouth was not named. The programme was shown on television late at night and there followed some controversy over the use of local school children as extras, although their contribution had been entirely innocent.

The film was made almost entirely at Sidmouth and the local population who weren't already tucked up in bed, would have been able to identify many local landmarks and locations where filming took place.

Miss Marple

Mystery novelist and playwright Agatha Christie was born at Ashfield Road in the Barton district of Torquay, and spent most of her latter days at Greenway on the Dart Estuary. It is therefore no mystery why, in her extensive writings, she should base many of her stories in the Devonshire landscape that she knew and loved so well.

The inscrutable Miss Marple is a Christie creation, a spinster detective

◄ *Joan Hickson (Miss Marple) scans the pages of the Exmouth Journal*

The stars of "Sleeping Murder" taking time off for a local social event

portrayed on the big screen by Margaret Rutherford but Joan Hickson has, in more recent times, made the part her own in the BBC televised stories partly 'made in Devon'.

A fifty strong production unit visited Devon for about a month in the summer of 1986. Several locations were used, including Otterton, Sidmouth, Lympstone, Starcross and Paignton. The sleepy town of 'Dilmouth' in the two-part *Sleeping Murder* featured much of the town and the sea front of Sidmouth and also Budleigh Salterton. The home of Colonel Hatchard-Smith in Cricketfield Lane, with its extensive views across the bay, was particularly suitable as the script called for sweeping views of the sea.

In the story a couple of newly weds buy the house of their dreams and the bride starts to wonder if it really is a 'dream house' as she has several experiences of 'deja-vu'. The couple set out to see if there is any substance to her feelings about the house.

In their investigations they visit the Lake District, which was actually a house near Ottery St Mary, and an asylum. The latter was the Western Counties Hospital at Starcross, which was also used as a police station for the filming. Any budding 'Miss Marples' who try to locate this building will, however, be disappointed as it was emptied and awaiting demolition at the time of filming and is now a housing estate.

The unit also filmed on the Torbay and Dartmouth Railway with, appropriately, some scenes shot as the steam train passed close to Agatha Christie's former home.

Another story in this short series was *Nemesis* which had a lot of the indoor action shot at the hotel on Burgh Island off Bigbury on Sea. The decor was perfect for the play and again was a most appropriate location as Agatha Christie stayed there several times. She is also believed to have written the novel "Ten Little Niggers" there, a title which became *And Then There Were None* for the film in the USA.

A Perfect Spy

John le Carre's international best selling spy books have been in great demand by film makers. Films have been made from "The Spy Who Came in From the Cold", "The Little Drummer Girl" and "The Looking Glass-War" and the BBC have adapted two other novels to make *Tinker, Tailor, Soldier, Spy* and also *Smiley's People*.

A Perfect Spy is regarded, by many, as the pick of the bunch and thankfully for us had large parts of it filmed in the Westcountry. The story-line centres on Magnus Pym, a vital member of the British Secret

Service who disappears after attending his father's funeral. Thus begins a manhunt for the 'Perfect Spy' while the spy himself hunts for his own identity. The search is packed with sexual and spying intrigue combined with psychological depth and social realism. The filming was done entirely on location and the plot is set in England, Wales, Corfu, Prague, Switzerland and Austria, and the USA.

The central character, Magnus Pym, is played by Peter Egan, an established actor with many roles under his belt, our favourite being 'Paul' the unintentionally irritating neighbour of Richard Briers in the comedy series *Ever Decreasing Circles. A Perfect Spy* also stars Ray McAnally, Peggy Ashcroft, Alan Howard, Jane Booker and Benedict Taylor.

Ever diligent in our quest for authentic details, we infiltrated our own not-quite-so-perfect spy onto the set in Dawlish where the final scenes were shot. Magnus Pym had turned up at a guest house in the small seaside resort tracked down by the police, CID and SAS. Fitz arrived on set at 7.30 pm, enjoyed an evening meal, exchanged his normal natty suit for an ill fitting policeman's uniform and waited for his twenty second flash of stardom. He waited and waited until, after a breakfast of chicken kiev,

An ordinary picture of a bus in Dawlish (Farleigh Abbot) but with traffic going the wrong way around a one-way system

with garlic perfumed breath, he eventually dashed past the camera followed by fifteen others, at three o'clock in the morning.

During the 'take' an amusing comment was overheard which highlights the fact that actors playing the role of SAS men are not quite as tough or resilient as the real thing: "Can you get a cushion? One of the SAS men has hurt himself, bless him!"

The action was shot near the railway station and, as it was still dark, very strong spot lamps were needed, many of which were located along the edge of the railway line which follows Dawlish sea front. It is interesting to note here that Dawlish has the only railway station in England which can boast the dual claim that it is both on the sea front and in the town centre.

British Rail officials were on hand for the entire shoot and maintained a watchful eye on the proceedings. Great care was taken by the film makers to make sure that passing engine drivers were not startled or blinded by the mission which was underway in deepest, darkest Dawlish. The same couldn't be said of the trains in return as they caused problems whistling through the night and necessitating a number of retakes.

Film makers invariably have to re-arrange places and Dawlish was no exception. The town became 'Farleigh Abbot' for the shoot as can be seen on the name sign of the local newspaper, more usually known as The Dawlish Gazette. And the one-way clockwise traffic system was reversed – which explains why the bus in the photograph is going the wrong way round!

A Horseman Riding By

The success of R.F. Delderfield's writing is highlighted by the number of his books that became television series, and the number of plays which became West End hits, almost all of them written beneath Devonshire skies. It was on a lonely afternoon walk over Muttersmoor, high above Sidmouth, that "A Horseman Riding By" was born, a venue which has yielded some well known hymns and poetry from other literary persons. This massive epic was so long that it ran to three books – "Long Summer Day", "Post of Honour" and "The Green Gauntlet". The story follows Paul Craddock, invalided out of the Boer War, who faced the daunting task of restoring the neglected country estate of Shallowford, nestling in a secluded corner of Devon's Sorrel Valley.

The author pointed out that no person or place was intended to

Holbeton, in the South Hams, which has been used for ''A Horseman Riding By'', ''Treasure Island'', ''International Velvet'' and ''Jessie''

represent real life but rather a race of people in a land of many 'Shallow-fords' in scores of 'Sorrel Valleys'. In its television adaptation, in keeping with the setting of the book, the BBC used several locations in South Devon concentrating on Holbeton for village scenes and Bowringsleigh, a large house near Kingsbridge, for the Shallowford country estate.

The 'Sorrell Halt' of the novel was 'played' by Staverton Bridge on the Dart Valley line. In one scene a suitcase was thrown from the train onto the platform. The dramatic effect of this action was rather diminished, however, when the suitcase burst open to reveal nothing but scrumpled up newspapers!

To Serve Them All My Days

"To Serve Them All My Days" reflected English school life at a time when millions of young men were being sacrificed in the carnage of the Western Front. A shell-shocked Welshman, David Powlett-Jones, arrives in Devon to re-build his life. The setting for this book is a remote public school on Exmoor and is based on the author's own experiences at West Buckland

School. (The names of several characters were close enough to real life ones to be recognised.)

The subsequent BBC TV series starred John Duttine as the school master in charge of boys barely his junior with an influence to control their destiny. The Headmaster, Algy Herries, was played by character actor Frank Middlemass, and a touch of romance was added by Belinda Lane, Kim Braden and Susan Jameson.

For the purposes of this book, the most memorable scene was a spectacular car crash. With a great build up of dramatic tension the two vehicles, one carrying the hero's wife and babies, are seen approaching from opposite directions. The cameras continually cut from one to the other, getting closer all the while until suddenly they meet in a fatal impact. However, the tragedy of the situation is rather lost on anyone recognising the two separate stretches of Dartmoor road each vehicle used for the sequence ... as they are about twelve miles apart!

Despite the licence of such interpretations this highly acclaimed series won a large and dedicated audience.

Diana

Filming at Drewsteignton for "Diana". The shop in the picture is just an ordinary cottage cleverly adapted for the day!

The success of the other two Delderfield adaptations prompted the BBC to make a third. "Diana" was again dramatised by Andrew Davies with much location shooting at Drewsteignton and around Chagford. It starred Kevin McNally as John Leigh and Jenny Seagrove as Diana, the daughter of the wealthy Gaylorde-Suttons.

Rural Drewsteignton was transformed into an even more rural village – all manner of animals appeared to run loose around the square – each one notching up a handsome little appearance fee. But even this caused problems as a great deal of time and effort was spent driving a whole herd of Friesian cows into place, and then somebody pointed out that, historically, there would have been no Friesians around, so the animals had to be withdrawn and replaced by a herd of Devons.

The strongest element in Ronnie Delderfield's literary works is the way he told his stories with humour and compassion, always managing to suggest his characters were close, personal friends. He achieved this by always structuring his working day to allow contact with varieties of people. He would religiously work from ten in the morning for three hours, then set aside the afternoon to mix with or observe people in a number of active pursuits before returning for another three hour long session commencing at six in the evening.

Lame Ducks

Staverton's railway station, on the Dart Valley line, is a far cry from Luton Airport but model/actress Lorraine Chase found it a lovely location for filming. Whether or not she said "Nice 'ere, innit?" about this part of the Dartmoor borderland country is not known. For the second series of *Lame Ducks* most of the filming was done in and around the Staverton area – the station having its name changed to 'Stutterton Stop'.

This BBC comedy series featured a number of unusual, misplaced characters who found themselves thrown together living in a disused railway station. Ansell (Brian Murphy), Maurice (Tony Millan), Mr Drake (John Duttine), Angie (Lorraine Chase), Tommy (Patric Turner) and Ray (Giles Cole) are the bunch of eccentrics who star in the series.

Between Ashburton and the densely populated urban area of Torbay is a land of narrow, twisting lanes, a rural backwater of small villages buried deep beneath a steep rolling landscape. It is an area probably quieter than Dartmoor as people content themselves in staying on the main highways which skirt it. The team took full advantage of this to film at many locations in the area. Landscove Church was used and for the television series it became Lower Bickshaw, whilst Buckfastleigh became Fennybrook Village.

The series was recorded in the summer of 1984 and was televised in five half-hour episodes.

Penmarric

This was another costume drama made in 1979 which was set in Cornwall but used the Dart Valley Railway for some 'steamy' scenes!

Rogue Male

A British aristocrat sets out to shoot Adolf Hitler as a reprisal for the murder of his fiancée by the Nazis – and almost achieves his objective. This TV film was based on a novel by Geoffrey Household and locations used in its making included the Dart Valley Railway and the Forge Tea Rooms at Holne on the edge of Dartmoor – both a far cry from Nazi Germany! The film was made in 1976 and starred Peter O'Toole, Alastair Sim, John Standing and Harold Pinter.

Roads To Freedom

Or, in the interests of this insertion, should it be 'Railroads to Freedom'? The BBC made thirteen 50-minute programmes in 1970 which serialized three Jean Paul Sartre novels of life, politics and defeat in France 1938-40. This was the first history/drama series to integrate real life characters like Chamberlain and Hitler and the actors involved included Daniel Massey, Georgia Brown, Rosemary Leach and Norman Rossington. Staverton's railway station on the Dart Valley line was where sequences showing people jumping out of a moving box van, presumably to freedom, were shot. (That is the sequences and not the people!)

Stocker's Copper

The Cornish consider themselves a separate race with their own language and if the River Tamar had been a mile longer, would have been completely cut off from the rest of Britain. Therefore it must have been almost an insult to dramatise a Cornish story on Devonshire soil. *Stocker's Copper* was set in Cornwall in 1913 and featured the relationship between a friendly policeman and one of the striking miners he was supervising. The

TV film starred Bryan Marshall, Jane Lapotaire and Gareth Thomas (later to become Blake in *Blake's Seven*). It was difficult to get more precise details of what was done in Devon in 1971 but the trusty old Dart Valley Railway was certainly used for filming as the Cornish are rather short of steam railways!

Edward The Seventh

The amount of work which went into the making of this superb piece of historical re-creation was well justified. The end result was a highly praised production of thirteen x 50-minute episodes chronicling the complete life of Queen Victoria's heir and the series won several awards. Made in 1975 it starred Annette Crosbie as Queen Victoria, Robert Hardy as Prince Albert, John Gielgud as Disraeli with Timothy West in the title role.

Many locations were used in this series including Oldway Mansion at

Timothy West (Edward VII) during filming at Oldway Mansion at Paignton

Paignton, so popular with the film makers. Oldway was needed as the exterior of the Hotel de Paris at Biarritz in SW France towards the end of Edward VII's reign in 1910. This fashionable resort on the Bay of Biscay has very little in common with Paignton, though it has about the same size population of about 30,000.

Oldway Mansion has been used as municipal offices for many years and its workforce has witnessed the comings and goings of many film crews. Largely the workers have learned to take the inconveniences in their stride, but problems of filming in a day to day working environment are inevitable. A healthy curiosity as to the proceedings is also to be expected so, to mask the eyes of curious typists peering out of the 'hotel', baskets of flowers were decked around all the windows. Outside red carpets, enormous polystyrene statues and other deceptive props combined to create the elite hotel setting amidst the council offices.

Local garage owner, Bill Rogers, was called upon to provide his prized Daimler for a scene. As he sported long sideboards at the time the film makers decided he looked just right to be the chauffeur of his own car. As he was not a member of Equity, he was given two hire fees for his vehicle instead!

Lady Nancy Astor

Oldway Mansion also became Nancy Astor's honeymoon hotel in Georgia.

These impressive statues in the foreground are made of polystyrene and kept blowing over!

Lisa Harrow and Piers Bronson at Oldway Mansion

Lisa Harrow played the part and her first husband was played on screen by Piers Bronson. A lot of decorative work was done to the exterior of Oldway and parts of it were barely recognisable.

Internally, imaginative and creative techniques were used. The entrance to the men's toilets was cunningly turned into the hotel reception area whilst opposite, the 'Ladies' entrance became the hotel bar.

Everything didn't go quite so smoothly externally when a large number of horses, being used for the filming, broke loose and ran wild over the grounds of Oldway early one morning.

Monty Python's Flying Circus

And now for something completely different ... a cult series which travelled through the offbeat into the bizarre exploring new and previously uncharted humour. 'Monty Python' was predictably unpredictable, its wicked wit verging on the sick (as opposed to being sick on the verge!) with jokes about dead parrots, upper class twits, a Ministry of Silly Walks, lumberjacks and so on. Between 1969 – 1974 forty-five episodes were screened, each scene ending abruptly either through a large cartoon foot clomping down on it from the skies, or from some other equally unrelated sudden stop to the proceedings.

The 'Circus' arrived in Devon to perform many sketches and the locations were so boringly ordinary that they could well have been filmed anywhere. A classic example was one entire episode which came from a Paignton Snack Bar, the only clue to it being a genuine Paignton snack bar was during the end titles when John Cleese took a bus ride to Babbacombe, talking from the upper deck of the open top bus.

Broadsands Beach, one of Britain's cleanest beaches, between Paignton and Churston, was selected for a sketch that might be recalled by 'Python' fans. It was filmed deliberately badly to give away how film makers create dramatic scenes. It started with library film of a large lion forcing its way through the undergrowth until it suddenly leaps high into the air above the camera. Next we see the obvious pretend lion (a man inside a lion costume) jumping down in front of the camera for a fight with a brave game hunter.

This was followed by a gigantic electric penguin with arms like tentacles terrorising all around it. If this wasn't enough, a cupboard, with ferocious teeth, came out of the sea and chased actress Carol Cleveland, a 'Python' regular, up the beach. Whilst being pursued she passes several large cactus trees. Each one removes a part of her clothing until she ends up topless, passing John Cleese at a desk (still on the beach) announcing "and now for something completely different..."

Fawlty Towers

The outrageously funny *Fawlty Towers* has been watched and enjoyed by millions of people all over the world. There were only two series ever made, the first six episodes in 1975 and the other seven episodes in 1979 and, despite much pleading and inducement, the writers John Cleese and Connie Booth wisely resisted the demand for more programmes. So there were only thirteen episodes in total, just enough to ensure they kept up a high standard without it becoming like so many tried and tested situation comedies which lose their sparkle through overkill.

Fawlty Towers is a hotel in Torquay, complete with its staff of misfits. There is Manuel (Andrew Sachs) who came from Barcelona to learn English, there is Polly (Connie Booth) the most 'normal' character who still gets drawn into awkward situations, and there is the viper-tongued Sybil (Prunella Scales), referred to by her husband as his 'little pet piranha fish'. The main character, of course, was Basil Fawlty (John Cleese) the manic manager who, in the course of trying to 'better' his clientele and hotel, only ever succeeded in sinking to greater depths whilst trying to extricate himself from embarrassing situations and what should have been fairly innocent activities.

The script for each half hour show was said to be twice the length of any 'normal' half hour sit-com, reflecting the fast and frenzied pace of both the quick and witty dialogue and the fast and farcical movements of the characters.

So how did it all begin? Life can certainly be funnier than anything dreamed up so most writers base their material upon true happenings and, in this case, John Cleese is no different to the rest of us. It was whilst he was with the 'Monty Python' team and filming in Torquay that he chose to stay at the Gleneagles Hotel in Asheldon Road, in the classy Wellswood district of Torquay. With a twist of exaggeration and some highly inspired

writing, he was to immortalise the owner and staff. When John Cleese returned to the hotel to consult his 'Basil Fawlty' in the early part of the 1970s he found that 'Basil' had gone to live in Florida. He revealed the source of his inspirations whilst participating in TV chat shows. And in February 1979 the Daily Express revealed that the real 'Basil' was in fact Donald Sinclair, a former Royal Navy Commander. Mr Sinclair protested that he was not as rude as Basil but his daughter confessed that she recognised him in the programme. Also there was a Spanish waiter, called Pepe, who only stayed for one season but was transcripted into one of the most engaging characters ever seen on television.

John Cleese has always shown great consideration towards the Gleneagles Hotel, expressing his concern that they shouldn't suffer as a result of *Fawlty Towers*. But the present owner considers that, if anything, it has helped the hotel as people come from all over the world to visit it. In fact, there are people who visited under the 'Basil' regime and, undaunted, still return each season to savour the delights of this hotel, which actually bears scant resemblance to the 'Fawlty Towers' seen on television.

The Gleneagles Hotel has certainly not exploited its situation (*Fawlty Towers* is not even mentioned in their brochure) but there have been other establishments around the county and throughout the country trading on the name of this fictitious hotel. To our knowledge there are hotels called 'Fawlty Towers' in Torquay, Sidmouth and Birmingham!

Although, initially, there were plans to film the series in Torquay, it was eventually decided to film in Oxfordshire or Berkshire, two counties with very short coastlines! But when the series was repeated on BBC2, it chalked up an amazing fourteen million viewers and helped to give Torquay a well deserved boost.

The Picnic

The Picnic was one of several silent comedy films made by the Two Ronnies – Corbett and Barker, the others included *Futtock's End* and *By the Sea*. Perhaps 'silent' is an inappropriate description as there was quite a lot of sound effects and much grunting and groaning going on, even though there was no actual dialogue.

The Picnic was 'Made in Devon' at locations around Dartington and Bovey Tracey and featured the disasters surrounding a fussy old general, his well-to-do family and their retinue of servants. The main location was 'Parke' at Bovey Tracey now the headquarters of the Dartmoor National Park. This fine old country mansion, built about 1820, was a perfect location with its fine open rolling parkland approaches.

This 30-minute television film was made in 1975 and also starred Barbara New, Madge Hindle and Patricia Brake, who incidentally had played Ronnie Barker's 'daughter' in both *Porridge* and *Going Straight*.

In order to recreate the right atmosphere, lorry loads of props were brought in, including all types of furniture and notably a very impressive four poster bed.

Dairyman Arthur Mann of Bovey Tracey was chosen to play the milkman who arrives at the door carrying a crateful of champagne instead of milk. To complete the scene of the milkman's delivery he also had to remove the empties. This was arranged by opening the bottles and pouring all the champagne straight down the sink! A couple of bottles were saved though, for the household to pour over their cornflakes, of course!

The 'Picnic' scenes were largely filmed beside the River Dart at Dartington, one particularly memorable scene involving a young lady with tight shorts and ample cleavage who, when bending over, attracted the attention of a Hereford bull. Another much used and exploited situation was shot in the gardens of a house in Bovey Tracey. A man innocently watering his garden was filmed from such an angle that it appeared he wasn't using a hosepipe!

31

Television Comedians

Kelly Monteith

The American comedian Kelly Monteith has a distinct line of patter looking at life's crazy but real situations and turning them into comedy. In his first television series for the BBC he showed great taste in choosing to come to Devon, concentrating on Torbay and Dartmoor, accompanied by actress Gabrielle Drake as his screen wife. He has since been back to the resort with his one man stand up show.

For some sequences in that original series they were supposed to be in a Mediterranean resort but locals who know their Tor Bay should easily have identified Broadsands Beach near Paignton.

A particularly memorable piece of 'deception' for anyone who recognised the disused garage at Haytor Vale was when the couple pulled into the garage and left the car in the hands of the attendant. On being told there would be quite a wait whilst work was being done on it, they made a polite enquiry about whether there were "any good antique shops around here". The garage owner pointed towards Haytor Rock and said there were "several just up the road". They must still be looking!

Little and Large

Each season Torbay manages to attract some top household names in the hope of filling its theatres each summer night. Some artists fill their time attending charity fund raising events and some also take the opportunity of filming sketches for their future television shows. Little and Large fall into this category having filmed extensively all around the Bay – notably St Marychurch – discreetly using out of the way locations so that no one would ever know they were there.

Dick Emery

The late Dick Emery was another comedian who was frequently spotted on the streets of Paignton, filming sketches for his television shows whilst he spent the summer in this lovely part of the world.

Spike Milligan

Spike Milligan visited Torbay to do some filming for at least one episode of his "Q" series. The Osborne Hotel in Hesketh Crescent, Torquay has a fine swimming pool backed by a classical crescent-shaped building. In this particular instance most male viewers could be forgiven for being distracted from the architecture as a host of attractive, topless models surrounded Mr Milligan by his 'Mediterranean' pool on the (English) Riviera.

The Saint

Between 1963 and 1968, 114 episodes of *The Saint* were recorded, starring Roger Moore as Simon Templar, the epitome of a suave sophisticated sleuth. The title came from his initials, 'ST', but surely his halo must have slipped over the deceptions perpetrated on us mere mortals? Admittedly in the 1960s not so many of us went on holidays abroad to exotic locations so perhaps we were not supposed to notice little details like the skyline of 'Monte Carlo' bearing a distinct resemblance to the Torquay Harbour front! Particularly obvious was the tallest building on the waterfront, which now houses DevonAir's Harbour Point studio. In those days it was the St James Hotel but, like Roger Moore, it is no longer a saint!

Worzel Gummidge

'Worzel Gummidge' is another character born in the pages of a book, who grew up to be a television star. The sinple minded scarecrow and assortment of odd friends was originally created by Barbara Euphan Todd, several decades ago, who wrote quite a few books about his adventures. Then he fell into the hands of Keith Waterhouse and Willis Hall, who write the television scripts, and also wrote some more books about him.

The television series was a product of the old Southern Television, but they chose Brixham as one of their locations. Filming in Brixham, in the summer of 1979, must have created problems all round as it was done during the peak of the holiday season, a time when Brixham becomes full to overflowing. Inevitably large crowds followed the action around from the harbour to the narrow back streets but the onlookers behaved impeccably. Unfortunately the same couldn't be said for the distant noisy lorries which ruined some of the initial attempts to shoot.

Jon Pertwee (Worzel Gummidge), Barbara Windsor (Saucy Nancy) and Una Stubbs (Aunt Sally) filming in the narrow streets of Brixham
◀

Jon Pertwee who played the title role was no stranger to Devon, having lived here for a period during his childhood. Guest star, bubbly Barbara Windsor, had also enjoyed many childhood holidays in Seaton and Beer in East Devon. She played the part of 'Saucy Nancy', a ship's figurehead, who trundled along Brixham's narrow thoroughfares on wheels rolling along on special rails. The third of the star trio to perform at Brixham however, Una Stubbs (or Aunt Sally), had never been to Devon before this filming took place, but she can be forgiven this minor indiscretion as it is generally believed that she was quite taken with the loveliness of the landscape.

Kidnapped

Kidnapped was based on the book of the same title by the Scottish author Robert Louis Stevenson (1850-1894) and featured historic events surrounding his native countryman Bonnie Prince Charlie (David McCallum of *Man from UNCLE* fame). This film was funded by three countries, an Anglo French German production which created some obvious communication problems. The lead actress was French and her voice had to be dubbed in Scottish and German, David McCallum could not speak French or German, and the German actor, Echort Bella couldn't speak English or French. The filming was described as 'slow' with a great deal of gesticulating evident!

The extras in this TV film had lots of fun being employed to lark around in the upper environs of a multi-masted ship. Aerial antics on the rigging earned them a bonus payment. Actor Patrick McNee was cast as a crusty old devil in the film and played the part of Balfour (incidently R.L. Stevenson's real name). 'Spud' Murphy, an extra with diverse maritime and nautical skills, was enlisted to shoot some scenes with the ageing star. In one scene the script demanded that Spud should row Patrick McNee and two other characters out to Zeba, a large vessel anchored just off Dartmouth Castle. The dinghy used for this sequence was obviously chosen for its visual appearance and not because of its seaworthiness as it leaked profusely. In addition to this handicap, Spud had to row from Stumpy Steps into the face of a stiff south westerly breeze against a fierce incoming Spring Tide.

In another scene in the same leaky, but authentic looking dinghy, Spud had to row the leading lady out to yet another boat. The actress was decked out in a flouncy skirt of several layers – as was the customary dress for ladies of that day – and as the boat filled with water so her skirts acted as a sponge, which left her feeling none too comfortable. The problem was compounded by a mixture of misdirection and underestimation, on the part of the Director, of the strength of the current on the incoming power-ful Spring Tide. On the first 'take' Spud was accused of being too relaxed and more effort was urged. He obliged by putting more effort into the job, but with such powerful elements behind him he shot through the water like a speedboat – the film crew only just managing to keep the boat in focus!

On another occasion, an eighteen stone German actor had to be rowed out into the estuary. Despite warnings from the rowers the director de-layed the final shot too long and the heavyweight actor was left high and dry on the mud. Sentenced to wade back through extremely deep mud, he was not entirely happy with the situation and gave vent of his feelings with an outburst of multisyllabic German swearing.

A vessel called 'The Marques' featured in this film and faced problems when its propeller dropped off in the middle of the Dart estuary. The 'Marques' also featured in *The Onedin Line* and that tale of old Cornwall, *Poldark*. However, it had a tragic end when it sank with the loss of nineteen lives.

Bayard's Cove in Dartmouth has a waterfront of great potential for filming eighteenth and nineteenth century settings. It was used for *The Onedin Line* as Liverpool and in *Kidnapped* it was transported further north to become a Scottish fishing village. To veil obtrusive items and to recreate the mood of West Coast Scotland artificial mist was manufac-tured. However, when the film crew went out to sea, a real mist descended upon Start Bay, and was so dense that they got lost. They called for absolute silence on board and, with cupped hands to ears, managed to detect children playing on the not so distant shores. They steered in the direction of the sounds and sighted land at Strete. Greatly relieved they set course along the line of the coast and cautiously steered back to Dartmouth.

The Master of Ballantrae

In June 1983 HTV made *The Master of Ballantrae* in conjunction with an American company. This version starred actor Michael York who was one of the 'Three Musketeers' in 1973 and one of the 'Four Musketeers' in 1974! Also notable was Timothy Dalton, better known for becoming the fourth James Bond. Originally written by Robert Louis Stevenson, the

Bayard's Cove, Dartmouth which has been used for numerous television programmes and films

television adaptation followed a film version made in Great Britain in 1953, starring the legendary Errol Flynn.

Dartmouth was the setting for this period piece and for some shots Bayard's Cove became a Scottish Harbour. To give an air of authenticity two clipper ships were used and featured strongly in the background. The TV crew made their base at the Royal Dart Hotel in Kingswear. Philip Spooner, a young self-employed carpenter, was working at the Royal Dart at the same time. He was so keen to become involved with the project that every time the director passed by he would immediately dramatically feign an agonising death, or quote a classic line like "Alas Poor Yorick ..." Philip's persistence paid off handsomely and he was given an extra's part, that of a Scottish nobleman. His big moment came when a crowd assembled to greet Bonnie Prince Charlie on his return to Scotland. This was shot on a quiet beach near Dartmouth. As the boat came in, a boisterous wave caught it at a crucial point and swept one of the other extras into the water. The crowd, on land, were treated to the comical sight of his bright red underwear protruding up from the water!

Meticulous detail was taken during the filming to avoid showing anything modern which might mar the mood or reduce the credibility of the setting. Consequently, whenever breaks were taken, a team of workers had to scour the beach for any signs of contemporary litter which may have floated in on the tide or have been blown in on the wind. Cigarette stubs, paper cups and a varied collection of flotsam and jetsum were removed each time. It would never do for the eighteenth century Bonnie Prince Charlie to step into a red and white striped twentieth century Kentucky Fried Chicken carton, now would it?

Smuggler

HTV must surely wish that Dartmouth was on the South Wales coast, as they have sent film crews to the town on numerous occasions to make films or plays. *Smuggler* was a half hour action series designed to cater for all the family. The action was set in 1802 and starred Oliver Tobias. As a former naval officer turned smuggler he enjoys many lively capers, and Dartmouth is the recipient of many ill gotten gains.

A sequel to this series, still starring Oliver Tobias as Captain Jack Vincent, was called *Adventurer*. This time they really pushed the boat out – as far as New Zealand and the South Seas Islands, spending two million pounds on it.

Oliver Tobias in the Dartmouth Arms at Dartmouth

The Ravelled Thread

This was a film made for television, based on the book of the same title, about gun running during the American War of Independence starring Jack Wild (the 'Artful Dodger' in *Oliver!*) and John Junkin. Some filming was done at Dartmouth, the two providing an excellent backcloth for yet another period piece.

'Spud' Murphy was fitted out in the costume of a sweep along with a boy assistant. Both were carefully dressed to look the part, taking longer to get ready for the shooting than any other character, only for the clip to end up on the cutting room floor!

The Bell Run

The number of programmes set in Scotland and filmed in the Dart Estuary is simply amazing. In this case the BBC's *The Bell Run* was set in and around Scotland's offshore oilfields and in places like Aberdeen, except in this case the 'Granite City of the North' was represented by Kingswear! The Royal Dart Restaurant was turned into 'The Wharf Room' restaurant. To emphasise its role of restaurant a huge plastic lobster was introduced. In addition to this there were plastic pork pies, plastic cheeses and rubber vegetables. Fitz worked on this scene as an extra, an event which took from 10.00 am to 7.10 pm, reduced to a mere three to four minutes of screen time, and his contribution eventually appearing as little more than an out-of-focus elbow seen from a great distance (you may recall it?)

In addition to the plastic props and rubber relics lying around the set, he also noticed very large jars of salad cream, eggs, loaves of bread and a mystery object. This transpired to be a perfect plastic model of an 'Eggs Benedict' (which turned out to be the star of the action that day). The actor and actress of the scene who visited 'The Wharf' were obliged to order some food if they wanted to enjoy a drink in the restaurant. They reluctantly ordered 'Eggs Benedict' which the man promptly tossed into the estuary. This simple piece of drama didn't go 'eggsactly' to plan and after several rehearsals and several takes, a small flotilla of Eggs Benedict could eventually be seen bobbing towards the open sea. These were duly retrieved, and attached to a fishing line lashed to a BBC props man rowing a small boat, ensuring that they drifted in the right direction. No wonder we hear so many jokes about the BBC canteen!

'Spud' Murphy of Kingswear, all dressed up as a chimney sweep, complete with apprentice—but victim of the cutting room floor

Five Go Mad in Dorset and Five Go To Mescalin

What do you get when you take four frightfully decent children (and a jolly nice dog) who are permanently on their 'hols' in the country or at the seaside and mix them with some stereo-type villains, some awfully exciting adventures (only stopping for regular and frequent picnics with lots of scrummy food) and a guaranteed happy ending? Enid Blyton knew the answer and used these ingredients to produce a recipe for success in a long, long string of 'Famous Five' adventure stories enjoyed by generations of children.

Channel Four's 'Comic Strip' team also recognised the winning formula and produced two parodies of these stories, *Five Go Mad in Dorset* (it was Devon) and *Five Go To Mescalin* . Set in the halcyon days of high summer our intrepid heroes bicycled out along quiet country lanes to sunny coastal beaches all beautifully capturing the Blyton mood – but in an amusing and entertaining way.

The Comic Strip's instantly recognisable characters needed very little exaggeration from Enid Blyton's originals. There was Julian, the eldest, Dick (who fitted his name), George (who didn't fit her name as she was actually a girl but preferred people to think she was a boy), Anne the 'baby' (who was only a 'silly girl') and of course lovable Timmy the Dog. Together they sallied forth to a background of cheerful 'housewife's choice' music through high hedged lanes, flanked by flowers, stopping for well-earned breaks to guzzle gallons of scrumptious ginger beer.

When the food that Aunt Fanny packed was well and truly demolished they would stop at a nearby farmhouse to buy lots more delicious goodies and maybe camp the night in the farmer's barn. It would be then they overheard a furtive conversation "... caves ... (whisper whisper) ... stolen goods ... (whisper whisper) ... midnight tonight ... (whisper whisper) ..." With curiosity aroused, so would begin another daring adventure. Poor old Timmy seems to come off worst in these spoof adventures as he gets poisoned at regular intervals – but of course all is well as the little bounder is soon seen trotting along in fine fettle in the next scene, completely recovered.

Five Go Mad in Dorset involved much chasing around the lanes of South Devon with a climax at Berry Pomeroy Castle, the most haunted castle in the West Country. *Five go to Mescalin* should have really been entitled "Five Go to the Great Mewstone" as the small island off the coast near Plymouth is where they actually filmed much of the episode. The Great Mewstone is a well known landmark to all who enter Plymouth. In 1830 it was occupied by Samuel Wakenham and his wife, and in the late 1920s it was given, as a wedding present, to the daughter of Lord

Chelmsford. Today it is an unpopulated, four acre target for the guns of the land based HMS Cambridge, near Wembury.

The locations for these two short comedy films were not generally known which is probably just as well as this golden stretch of coastline from Prawle to Plym remains a largely unspoilt haven for those who like to get away from it all to have their own adventures.

Jessie

Bigbury on Sea was a location for a Play for Today called *Jessie*. It was a period piece set in Victorian times and included Nanette Newman, Nigel (*Yes Minister*) Hawthorn and Annette Crosbie, who can claim the distinction of receiving BAFTA awards for having portrayed two Queens of England, Catherine of Aragon and Queen Victoria (but not in the same programme!)

The play was about a girl called Jessie who was hired to look after the son of the Lord of the Manor. The son could not communicate, probably for some deep psychological reason, but developed an affinity with Jessie. But when she fell in love with the groom she was dismissed, an act which so brutally affected her charge, that it stirred him to break his silence.

John Weeks was enlisted as an extra, and dressed in full Victorian regalia, for this play. His appearance was made complete by a large moustache, so typically sported by the gentlemen of the day. Alas for poor John, when the cameras were ready to roll he gave an almighty sneeze and blew the moustache right off! Fortunately the make up girl was on hand to stick it back into position.

On another occasion the coach carrying all the costumed actors and extras was held up in the narrow main street of Holbeton, just outside the village school. The children were somewhat startled to see such an entourage, ladies with bustles, men with bristling moustaches, bowlers and stiff collars. They all looked larger than life as they were all fully made up, and were therefore an unexpected entertainment, albeit for a few fleeting moments, for the children of a quiet South Hams village school. As the coach cranked into gear before moving off. John turned towards the children and, through the window, suddenly pulled the ugliest face that he could muster. Fortunately, unlike the real Victorians, they were amused!

Later, at Holbeton the villagers got to see much more of the stars as an elaborate set was erected near the Mildmay Colours, a pub which was featured in *International Velvet* also starring Nanette Newman!

Outside the inn a Victorian market scene was created and many old fashioned market stalls were brought in. Modern street appendages like lampposts were disguised by massive branches which hid them from view. Large amounts of sand and soil were liberally dumped giving an authentic air to the proceedings, though not everything was false. At the village shop the original bake house was used and the exceedingly nice cakes and bread on show were all genuine. Outside and around the village, hens and ponies were let loose to give a splended backcloth to the action.

Jamaica Inn

Dark events on the Cornish coast eh? Even darker events on Dartmoor! In the autumn of 1982 HTV made a film not on Bodmin Moor, home of the legendary inn of the title, but high on Northern Dartmoor, some twenty-five miles from the original setting.

Daphne du Maurier immortalised this inn in her famous novel about Mary Yellan (Jane Seymour), a young girl forced through circumstances to go and live with her downtrodden aunt (Billie Whitelaw) and rough, drunken uncle Joss (Parick McGoohan) whom she soon learns to fear and hate. On the bleak desolate moors she becomes involved with smuggling and murder before finally surrendering to the attractions of her uncle's brother, Jem (Trevor Eve) and riding off into the sunset with him.

Jamaica Inn is a real pub situated on the road across Bodmin Moor at the small hamlet of Bolventor. Many people imagine the inn to be just a stone's throw from the coast but in reality it is some eleven miles in a straight line to Port Isaac Bay on the North Cornish coast. Some have even tried it on horseback to see if it is a feasible jaunt. In this film adaptation a crowd of horse riders leave the 'inn', ride over Hound Tor (similar to many of the tors on Bodmin) and arrive at the coast in an instant. Such a feat on Bodmin is impossible, and on Dartmoor it is simply beyond belief!

Jamaica Inn, on a main highway, now the A30, was always a meeting place for rogues but has developed from a staging inn to become a tourist attraction. Unfortunately its popularity with the visitors has meant much twentieth century development including spacious car parks etc. rendering it totally unsuitable for portraying the nineteenth century inn.

This minor problem was soon solved – a full scale fibre glass and timber facade was constructed on the Artillery ring road which runs southwards from Okehampton into the wilderness of Northern Dartmoor, at a spot called New Bridge. Six men were employed to build it and the specifications had to allow for the extremes of Dartmoor weather. At one stage a substantial part of the roof blew off, an occurrence which prompted even more stringent measures to shore up the facade for the week it stood on the wrong moor. Plastic sheets were put down to allow chippings to be laid

Jamaica Inn on Dartmoor!

around the building, and then they were carefully rolled up after filming was finished – you would never have known it had been there! The dismantled shell was reassembled in Gloucestershire around another pub whose interior was deemed perfect for indoor filming.

Further sequences were shot at Hound Tor and at Bonehill Rocks, on the hillside above Widecombe. Most of the coastal shots were filmed at Polzeath on the Cornish coast, so the stars opted to stay at Yelverton on SW Dartmoor, well sited for visiting either of the two main filming areas.

The series was shown in three parts and certainly captured the mood of Bodmin Moor, even though it was really Dartmoor!

A Winter Harvest

This is one of the few films featured in this book which is both set in and filmed in Devon. The BBC had an idea to make a film based on a year in the life of a Dartmoor hill farm, and playwright Jane Beeson, who is married to a Dartmoor farmer and therefore well qualified in such matters, wrote a 'drama documentary' entitled *A Winter Harvest* . The story is strictly fictional and relates how Caroline, a town girl, marries a Dartmoor farmer and, after six months of mixed marital blessings, finds herself facing the running of the farm whilst her husband goes to hospital for an operation.

The lead role was played by Cheryl Campbell who threw herself wholeheartedly into her attempts to cope with the farm chores and there were several occasions when a serious accident could so easily have happened. In one shot 'Caroline' had to drive a tractor down a steep slope and the brakes failed. The film crew started to panic as she drew closer but she managed to slam it into reverse, dramatically skidded to a halt, and found that she'd knocked the camera over and had to retake the shot! On another occasion 'Caroline' was called upon to scale a high silo tower which Cheryl Campbell insisted on attempting herself. John Earle, a famous mountaineer and film maker, was 'roped in' to assist in the shoot and, hidden from camera view, he ensured she was attached to a well concealed safety rope.

As befits the peace of the Dartmoor environment, the action is slow moving and the plot simple using many moorland shots, but creating an atmospheric feel to the rural proceedings. Most of the scenes were filmed on two farms near Manaton, the latter featuring in a scene at a 'fayre' with a hang-glider flying in over the church, a flower show, sideshows and a wellie throwing competition as Caroline simply browsed in the warmth of some rare Dartmoor sunshine. The three 50-minute episodes covered the changing seasons and some of the winter scenes were filmed in the heat of a warm summer. Poor Cheryl Campbell was obliged to wrap up warmly in heavy woolly garments whilst the temperatures soared beneath a blazing sun.

At nearby Haytor the geographical accuracy of the script was borne out as it was claimed that Teignmouth could be seen in the distance – as indeed it can on a clear day. But there was a little deception when the husband, played by Mark Wing-Davey (noted for his role as the double-headed Zaphod Beeblebrox in *Hitchhiker's Guide to the Galaxy*), went to hospital in Exeter. No he didn't! This was filmed at the Polish Hospital at Stover, just outside Newton Abbott.

The Gable family at Moretonhampstead found their encounter with the film crew to be quite an eye

The stars and friends of ''A Winter Harvest'' taking time out to relax

45

opener. Peter, their 10 year old son, was a pupil at Moretonhampstead's Junior School when he was invited to have a part in *A Winter Harvest*. As he was so young the regulations demanded that he be chaperoned. His mother was thus employed to chaperone her own son for a fee of £20. The director and his assistant called on the family to ask if they could film a short scene, where Caroline calls on the wife of the farmhand who has been helping her out, using their kitchen. They agreed and then were amazed at the scale of operations needed to capture just a few minutes of film time. Although only the kitchen was needed, the whole house was taken over, an outside caravan and the upstairs were used for changing rooms, and twenty-nine people were on the set for about eleven hours to record just two minutes. However the Gable Family were unanimous in their praise of this particular film crew and were more than pleased to go out for a meal with them afterwards.

Like most programmes *A Winter Harvest* received mixed reviews although it gained quite a following, and rated the biggest audience for such a drama series in 1984. There was talk of a sequel series but it was found to be impossible to re-assemble the same cast so the idea was dropped.

The Country Diary of an Edwardian Lady

Edith Holden's book of this title is in the "Guinness Book of Records" having sold more than two million hard back copies in the UK alone. It has also been translated into fourteen foreign languages and, almost inevitably, been made into a television series. It has been the most successful English language publication in the last twenty-five years.

Central Television produced a twelve part serial, one for each month of the year, to show the events which Edith Holden experienced as chronicled in the beautifully illustrated country diary. Pippa Guard played the part of Edith Holden in this television series.

The series is set in 1906, a mixture of dramatising the artist's life and portraying the country life and cycle of nature that she recorded. It features many flashbacks which included a visit to Devon which she made in the Spring of 1902. As usual she arrived complete with all her painting equipment to stay at the small Dartmoor borderland village of Dousland near Yelverton. Over the next eight years she returned many times having developed an affinity with the landscape and having established many friendships with the local population. The series was faithfully filmed using many of the locations from the County Diary. The valley of the River Plym between Dartmoor and its estaury, was used for filming. Huckworthy Bridge near Walkhampton was of special significance as

Edith Holden did an oil painting of it as a wedding present for her great friend, Belle Trathen.

Sadly Edith Holden was killed in a bizarre drowning accident at Kew, in 1920. She was only forty-nine years old and her precious diary of 1906 which was stored away, remained undiscovered for seventy years. The book was published by the Exeter publishers Webb and Bower who had the foresight to realise that they had an outright winner on their hands.

Alien In The Family

It is a long way from the distant planet of Galgonqua to the woods of Lydford in Devon but when a spaceship landed on Ringmoor Down, high on the hill above Meavy on the south western side of Dartmoor, the two places became inextricably linked. This six episode children's adventure serial is a simple, everyday tale of how a young boy called Bond (Grant Thatcher) embarks on a journey to find his long lost sister and, with the help of an Earth family, eventually locates her inside a transistor radio in a junk shop!

The programme is based on a novel by New Zealander Margaret Mahey and a month of location filming was done in West Devon and Exeter. Despite the wet weather encountered, the crew kept to schedule and they all appreciated filming in such glorious locations.

The Beatles' Magical Mystery Tour

Although it is hard to imagine a better place than the South West to join a 'Magical Mystery Tour', this particular journey was not at all well received by the critics, giving them a distinct bout of travel sickness. Perhaps the unfortunate timing of the film making in September 1967 had something to do with its poor performance as the Beatles' manager, Brian Epstein, had committed suicide just prior to it.

The Beatles were no strangers to Devon having visited Torquay before their spectacular rise to stardom in the 1960s, on 28 October 1964 they performed at Exeter's ABC Cinema and the following night entertained more hysterical and delirious fans at the ABC in Plymouth.

After several planning sessions, the Beatles left London to join the Fox and Hayes coach (URO 913E) at Teignmouth. The tour hostess on the bus 'Wendy Winters', was played by Mandy Weet who chaperoned the Fab Four on an eventful tour of the Moor. Their attempts to get to Widecombe Fair were thwarted by a road bridge which proved to be too narrow for the bus – even with the help of transcendental meditation! The resulting traffic jam was so horrendous that the entire ensemble retreated to Plymouth for a hearty lunch in the Berni Steak Bar at the Grand Hotel. The entourage then moved out of Devon and on to Bodmin and Newquay to complete the fiming. The inside scenes were later filmed inside massive aeroplane hangars at West Malling in Kent.

Tales Of The Unexpected

An episode of this series was called *The Boy Who Talked to Animals* (not David FitzGerald talking to Gus Honeybun!).This was about a boy who befriended a turtle and went to sea on it. The impression given was that it was filmed on a golden beach in the tropics. It was filmed on one of the beaches in breezy Barnstaple Bay!

Shoestring

Eddie Shoestring was a fictional private detective employed by the fictional radio station, Radio West, to solve its listeners' problems. Although this was a Bristol-based thriller series, some of the twenty-six episodes, shown in 1979-80, were shot further west like at Saunton Sands where Shoestring (Trevor Eve) was almost blown away by the incessant on shore breeze.

Knowing that some viewers will always try out a phone number if they hear one on television, producers are usually very careful about phone numbers given on screen. But by a strange co-incidence, when the fictional Radio West gave out its number, people who tried ringing it found themselves talking to a real independent radio station in Plymouth! Unfortunately, as Eddie Shoestring worked for a rival station, they were unable to help with the listeners' detective queries.

Mogul

Long before the days of *Dallas* the BBC had its own long-running series about an oil company. John Elliott based his series upon his observations of BP and, although it ran to around eighty episodes, it remained good entertainment. It did, however, change its name to *The Trouble-shooters* in this country, staying as *Mogul* everywhere else. Starring Robert Hardy, Ray Barratt, Geoffrey Keen and Philip Latham it featured the internal workings of a large company with various struggles for power.

Several episodes were filmed over the extensive dunes and beaches of Saunton Sands in North Devon. No doubt this made a convincing Middle East or desert landscape, when it wasn't pouring with rain!

Drake's Venture

John Thaw, alias 'Regan' from *The Sweeney*, came to Devon after completing fifty-two episodes of playing the tough cop in the crime series, to take on the mantle of playing Sir Francis Drake, an Elizabethan tough guy. The film was made by Westward TV in 1979 in and around the coast of Devon. Plymouth Sound and the cliffs near Strete were prominent maritime locations whilst Sydenham House was used for indoor action. Queen Elizabeth was portrayed by Charlotte Cornwall, and she had two dogs which behaved perfectly all over Sydenham House, except in one particular spot which is supposedly haunted!

The story details Drake's greatest venture, a mission to bring back untold treasures, to boldly go where no man has gone before (does this begin to sound familiar?). Without ever leaving our coastal waters the story of Drake crossing the Atlantic, through Magellan's Strait and around Cape Horn is unfolded. But adventure is never plain sailing and mutiny threatened. Thomas Doughty, an old friend of Drake, was executed on the cliffs a few miles from Dartmouth, for plotting and conspiracy. The technicalities of the execution gave rise to much discussion amongst the 'extras' and bystanders who were pusszled over why so much effort was spent on making the executing block look 'old' when at the time it would probably have been a brand new construction made from South American timber!

With great attention paid to detail, a replica of Drake's own ship, the Golden Hind, was used but it nearly didn't make it. In fact filming was delayed for two weeks when, in true Elizabethan fashion, it was actually hi-jacked in the Red Sea whilst en route to Devon!

A major problem in filming at sea is that the camera crew are usually mere landlubbers who are ill used to the roll and pitch of sea going vessels. For this programme many of the cameramen suffered from chronic sea sickness, not helped by the memory that one of their colleagues, when filming the return of Sir Francis Chichester, actually died from an extreme sea sickness bout.

Local radio presenter and disc jockey John Pierce was an 'extra' for this film. He was kitted out as an Elizabethan gentleman and was one of a group in the background for several sequences. As part of his costume he

Charlotte Cornwell (Queen Elizabeth I) complete with treasures in "Drake's Venture"

was required to wear thigh length boots (try saying that quickly!) Anyone who has ever observed Mr Pierce in the flesh will know that he is a very tall lanky individual, his height emphasised by his crane like legs. He recalls how he was required to pose with the camera shooting upwards, a trick which always 'lengthens' the subject. On this occasion, at an opportune moment, John lowered his thigh boots to his knees and for all intents and purposes appeared to have legs about ten feet long!

Treasures Of The Mindlord

This was an ambitious project for our local television company, Television South West. The seven part series was a computer-based quiz featuring some unusual Intergalactic characters. There was Eynon, the Mindlord of One Thousand Stars (the celestial type), a dotty wizard, a pun dropping dwarf called To-lar (who wasn't short on wit), an assistant to the Mindlord called Minyon and 'Kerna' – a computer (with a positively Cornish sounding name), believed to be the most complex computer in the Universe (or so it modestly thought). This collection of characters was given a single mission, after transporting the Earthlings through time and space, to test their suitability for becoming members of the Mindlord's Intergalactic Confederation. Competing in pairs, two teams of children were put through a labyrinth of tests and time tricks.

The reason for the inclusion of the programme in this book is that the filming of the series was done in some very exotic locations. No expense was spared as the children were transported across the Universe to the disused Breakwater gas works at Cattedown in Plymouth! Other locations included the Theatre Royal, a local nightclub, an old manor house and a thirteenth century farmhouse. Most of these still remain in our universe but the gasworks has been demolished – or has it been teleported to a distant galaxy with a greater need for one?

Programmes of this nature require great technical expertise to ensure that they run smoothly, particularly in cases like this, filmed without the

Intergalactic Visitor, Mike Edmonds (Tol-Ar) in "Treasures of the Mindlord"

luxury of a re-take. Once it began there was no turning back, even when problems of communications arose with thick walls or heavy rain. The actors (or intergalactic visitors as they preferred to be thought of) worked to a crucial time allocation for each team and had to be primed to be equally fair to each contestant. As in Channel 4's *Treasure Hunt*, the cameramen and sound technicians were obliged to follow the children around with hand held cameras, the contestants not always taking the right route. Although each game took only six and half minutes, the programme took three days in the editing room and another day in dubbing. Wouldn't you have thought that the Mindlord could have lent a helping hand here?

Some Day Man

The semi-sterile modern streets of Plymouth have also been used for fliming. *Some Day Man*, a Channel Four production, featured 'Mik O'Reardon' (Joseph Marcell) a black Jamaican resident in England who wasn't prepared to take a job where he would be expected to start 'at the bottom'. One day opportunity knocks for him when a coloured stranger calls at his door with the offer of a top executive job with a large organisation. When he arrives on his first day, he finds that he has been there for years and is one of the established staff, with his own office complete with ongoing affair with his secretary. He soon finds that life isn't quite so easy at the top, faced with a string of crises, making decisions on subjects he knows nothing about, and coping with an irate wife demanding divorce over an affair he hasn't actually had. So is it a dream? Is it a nightmare? Or is it voodoo?

The making of *Some Day Man* posed its own peculiar problems. To interpret a West Indian Fable, penned by an Australian writer, produced by a white Englishman and located in Plymouth, created a tough challenge to the production team. Plymouth, unlike many British cities, does not have a thriving ethnic community so it was necessary to bring in West Indian extras from St Paul's in Bristol. The filming was done during the coldest days of January and the West Indian extras had a difficult time trying to get to Plymouth through the snowy and icy weather. However, some of the few local West Indian residents were employed having received special dispensation from Equity.

Of the eleven locations used the most problems occurred with a deserted restaurant on the top floor of the Civic Centre. A small fortune was paid out on extra thick materials to mask the floor to ceiling glass windows as the brilliant January sunshine was too strong even for a West Indian based

David Rogers interviewing Joseph Marcell in sub-zero temperatures in Plymouth's city centre

idea, and the roaring winds were so forceful that the original neutral density material rustled and crackled too loudly.

Location filming was also done on the Belliver Estate, at the Armada Centre, on the City Streets (Sunday shooting in sub zero temperatures) – and in Studio One where a terrace house set was constructed.

When a West Indian nightclub was needed for filming, scouts were sent to scour Bristol and Southampton for the right location. They needn't have looked any further than out of the window of their headquarters in Plymouth – "Ziggy's" was perfect for their needs.

Some Day Man was billed as a comedy and part fantasy – a West Indian fable filmed in Siberian conditions but 'Made in Devon'.

TV Commercials
Made In Devon

Motor Vehicles

When a new car is launched it must, through its brief commercial, show us that it is well able to cope with all sorts of hazardous road conditions. The new, gleaming model assumes the role of film star for the duration of the advert and is required to perform, demonstrating all the heroics, style, panache and swashbuckling excitement of SuperCar in its battle across hostile country, through storm and tempest, against alien environmental forces, all designed to test every facet of its road worthiness. Devon's notorious roads lend themselves admirably for this task and have been used by at least four major car manufacturers. Dartmoor in particular can be a real swine, with its sinuous roads, its switchback hills, its errant animals and its temperamental weather providing the perfect challenge for any car.

The Ford Sierra, when it first appeared, was thus challenged to triumph over Dartmoor terrain and a helicopter acted as a photographic spy to capture the car's various capabilities on film. Great attention to detail was paid as the carefully edited commercial showed scenes from around the Moor, all many miles apart, which eventually rolled together into one apparently continuous journey. The long undulating straight from the edge of Chagford Common to Warren House was followed by the steeply plunging and highly dangerous chicane that climbs from Poundsgate toward Sherberton Common. If we could buy the car capable of roaming so far afield in so short a time it would indeed be a new concept in vehicular transport.

Ford used Dartmoor for another important advertisement – a celebration of an anniversary of the company. The History of Ford commercial was filmed at Haytor and involved some extraordinary arrangements. Various models from the past were taken to the rocks and winched into position atop a granite shelf near the main rockpile. We are of course referring here to the vehicular type with the classy chassis and the big bumpers and not the leggy lovelies with the classic cleavage and the big boobies so frequently used to sell cars! Water cannons were used to spray the cars to make them shiny and gleaming. Being about 1500 feet above sea level caused a few problems here because the water pressure from one fire tender was not sufficient to give a dramatic enough spray, so another fire tender was installed to boost the supply. A Spitfire was used to create an atmospheric effect and a film crew captured it all from a helicopter. Unfortunately a great deal of damage was done to the paths leading to the tor and it was this which prompted the National Park Authority to review their attitudes towards film crews and filming on the moors.

There was a different make of brand new car, whose name we dare not mention, which also came to Devon to have its promotional film and television commercial made. The cameras were all set up, the briefings were completed, the clapperboard was poised to snap shut, it was 'all systems go' – except the car wouldn't start! A frantic producer and crew had to push it to get it going. Had this 'out take' been kept the caption could have claimed "0-60 in about half an hour".

Yet another car to travel over hill and dale, at an apparently supersonic speed, was the Rover 213. In the space of a thirty second commercial it

Filming the Ford Sierra commercial at the Warren House Inn on Dartmoor

could be seen whizzing over Bodmin Moor in Cornwall and then speeding through the narrow lanes of the South Hams past Yealmpton, Bigbury and Hope Cove. Thirty miles in thirty seconds means 3,600 miles per hour. That would work out at 2966.52 miles per hour faster than Richard Nobel's 'Thrust II'. And all this at over forty miles to the gallon!

Another classy car advert to combine the natural beauty of a Devonshire sunrise and the man made beauty of what appears to be an exclusive, jet set nightclub, was one which was done for Toyota. The night club, apparently somewhere like Monte Carlo, was in fact council offices. Not that Oldway Mansion at Paignton, the former home of the Singer (sewing machine) family are any ordinary council offices. The magnificent building was wonderfully illuminated but the eye was led away from the building by an elegant and beautiful lady who slinked into the car, which is, after all, where the manufacturers wanted our eyes to go!

You may also recall an advert with a gigantic dining room and enormously long dining table – so long, in fact, that the butler had to get in his nifty little Fiat and drive from end to end to serve the Lord or Lady of the house. The opening scenes to this advert were shot at Oldway Mansion but, although the ballroom is certainly an ample size, the interior scenes were shot elsewhere.

It is appropriate that car manufacturers should choose Oldway Mansion

Twiggy branching out on motorcycle in the narrow streets of Dartmouth

as a backcloth to their car advertisements as, in 1906, Paris Singer was the first person, other that Mr Rolls or Mr Royce, to own a Rolls Royce car.

A leading firm of Japanese motorcycle manufacturers chose Twiggy as the perfect person to show off their range of motorcycles. In their commercial Twiggy had to ride various mopeds in and around Dartmouth's quaint, narrow streets, which is so much easier on a 'nippy' little motorcycle than trying to negotiate tricky turns in a cumbersome car!

One of the lower ferries at Kingswear was taken out of service for half a day while Twiggy was filmed coming off it and up the slip road into town. We talked to many people who met Twiggy on her brief visit to Dartmouth, and they were unanimous in their opinion that she was a lovely lady in every respect. In fact not one person would have wanted her to 'get on her bike' – even though she did over thirty times!

Perhaps the next best thing to an advert actually 'Made in Devon' is an advert inspired by an incident in Devon. David Knowlings, longest serving train driver with the Dart Valley Railway, was unwittingly instrumental in creating the idea for a short series of TV commercials.

It must have been 'one of those days' for Dave as he happily played about with a large road haulage traction engine in the station yard at Buckfastleigh. The problem with 'The Pride of Leven' was that it lacked a brake and, like space rockets, had to go into reverse in order to stop. Whilst performing the tricky manoeuvre of parking this wondrous vehicle in its shed, it suddenly slipped out of gear.

Some time later, Dave was in the uncomfortable position of having to inform his boss that he had 'some good news and some bad news'. Yes, he had managed to get the traction engine into the shed, but his bosses car now had a flat battery, in fact he also had a flat car!

Those who were not directly involved saw the amusing side of the incident and Dave himself is quite philosophical about this occurrence as he maintains that it's just as well the car was there as he could have gone through the wall of the station!

Thus it was that an MG Sports car, parked in front of the railway buildings, suddenly flattened by the might of the traction engine created the perfect situation for a well known insurance company to make a drama out of a crisis.

Other Products

It is hardly surprising that when the landscape creates a steep gorge, clothed by beautiful woodland, blessed by a lovely moorland river crossed by an attractive stone bridge, that film makers see it as an idyllic setting to make commercials. Fingle Bridge is such a spot and has been used for at least ten television commercials, some of which were filmed exclusively for overseas audiencess. R.D. Blackmore, who wrote "Lorna Doone", proclaimed it to be the best beauty spot in England. The film makers have endorsed this, using clever camera angles and zoom lenses in the cause of promoting various items such as yoghurt.

The production crew only had a single day to shoot this commercial and a scene in high summer was demanded. Alas the day they chose in May was as miserable and cold as only a Dartmoor day could be. However, 'the show must go on' so the 'Full of Fitness' family duly arrived. The finished product was to show the family, all dressed in white, crossing the Teign on stepping stones to enjoy an idyllic picnic on the banks.

In the film industry, thirty seconds can seem to last a lifetime, particularly when the cast are dressed for summer on a freezing day. Between the summery shots, 'Mum' was seen to don her large fur coat and disappear inside the Angler's Rest to consume brandies. The children of this TV commercial family, however, were praised by spectators for their perfect behaviour and sheer stalwart attitude in the face of a bitterly cold, damp wind, all in the course of promoting yoghurt.

But Fingle Bridge has its fine days too and when they occur it is not only film makers who arrive but scores of visitors. A British Airways 'Fly the Flag' commercial, made for Australian consumption to challenge Quantas, was filmed there on such a day and provided some excellent free entertainment for the visitors.

The scene involved a vicar riding the sort of old fashioned bicycle that vicars ride. The chosen actor was one who had been used in so many television commercials as a vicar that it was second nature to him to go about his 'parochial business' in front of a host of cameras. At a given signal he had to weave through some parked cars and cross Fingle Bridge. Sat on the bridge was a leggy blond to whom the vicar pays homage by doffing his straw hat. As he reaches the end of the bridge an overhead aeroplane distracts him further and he tumbles from his cycle. Many unsuspecting onlookers later enquired at the nearby Angler's Rest whether or not the local rector had recovered from his mishap. He was obviously a most convincing actor. Praise the Lord!

In yet another commercial a camera was sited high on Prestonbury Castle, an ancient Iron Age Earthwork, which rises almost cliff-like above Fingle Bridge. Deep down in the valley, hundreds of feet below, a microscopic dot on the bridge is zoomed in on, to reveal a flautist playing his flute (what else?). The effect is stunning, the great range of the zoom creating an amazing shot. This was a commercial for Warwick Records making a compilation of romantic songs for one of their LPs.

Jack Price, the well known living legend of Fingle Bridge, has seen all

(left pic) The large plastic fish is caught! (right pic) Paul Hogan enjoys a glass of lager at Clovelly

manner of comings and goings with film crews and has been duly impressed by their code of professional conduct in utilising this beauty spot. There have also been many leading pop groups who, in the course of making promotional videos, have stopped off, shot several sequences and disappeared into the night leaving no trace behind.

Drewsteignton lies less than a mile fron Fingle Bridge and its quaint cottages and attractive square have been used by film makers for various purposes. A most unlikely commercial, which was made only in part there, was one for North Sea Gas. A cottage called Rockwood was externally converted into a pub called 'The Bay Tree', the sign being borrowed from a motel a few miles away. For the inside shots a pub in Dorset was used. In another scene a jogger is shown running past some 'olde worlde' cottages. This involved so many 'takes' that, by completion, the poor jogger was well and truly exhausted!

When Paul 'Crocodile Dundee' Hogan came to Devon it wasn't to wrestle with large amphibious reptiles of the lizard kind. The Aussie comedian visited Clovelly in North Devon to make one of a series of celebrated advertisements for Foster's lager. If you look carefully at the picture of the anglers on the harbour wall, you will no doubt think it strange that they should be fishing when the tide is out – but minor details such as this is no stumbling block to the clever film maker. We can assure you that in this scene, despite the lack of water, a real fish was caught. It was kept in a container in the boat in the picture! As live fish aren't the most patient of actors when it comes to tedious rehearsals, it had its own stand-in – a large plastic fish. This was just as well as, on the day the commercial was filmed, it was so hot that the poor chap entrusted with keeping the fish alive could barely keep himself awake. The heat also caused problems for the human extras because when the time came for the final takes, they had to be decked out in heavy fishermen's pullovers. No doubt after the filming was completed they were ready to down a few pints – I wonder which brand they chose?

A Prize Pub

"We've made so many dreams come true for you, folks ... but this time we are granting the wish of a lifetime ... The Sun is offering you a fabulous chance to win your own COUNTRY PUB ... It has a thatched roof and roses round the door. There's a popular public bar, a warm and cosy snug and a leafy beer garden ..."

The prize consisted of the tenancy of a pub under an eleven-year lease, a £5,000 float for the till, a manager's training course and an opening night

A double-take of the same pub in Pinhoe, Exeter,
A Place in the Sun—A Place in the Snow

party with 'Page 3' girls pulling the pints! All the contest required was to telephone a given number, and solve a pub puzzler each day for five days. Assuming that the masses could not resist such a tempting prize, BT must have rubbed their hands with glee at the digits clocking up!

And so it was in early September 1986 that a coach full of extras (a more trendy bunch of 'locals' than the real thing), were shipped in to Exeter along with a film crew, sports personalities Eric Bristow and Alex 'Hurricane' Higgins, and even three 'page 3' girls. A new temporary beer garden was hastily created with continental style tables and sunshades, and the front of the pub was garlanded by hanging baskets and several well stocked window boxes. With well chosen camera angles, a surfeit of cleavage behind the bar, and some clever production, The Heart of Oak in neighbourly Pinhoe became, for one afternoon, "A Place in the Sun" – the perfect prize for a lucky Sun reader.

The TV commercial went out a week after shooting and sparked much media attention with many other newspapers trying to put the whole thing into perspective (in other words – put in the literary boot!). Editorials abounded and headlines screamed "Fake" – could this attractive and desirable little countrified hostelry be the same real-life run down, dingy and dusty urban pub full of unfriendly and hostile natives?

Hostile natives? The Barber family took exception to this having lived in Pinhoe for many years, knowing it to be an extremely friendly community with its own unique village atmosphere. However, we locals were rather concerned about the happy 'customer' in the advert, seen carrying a tray full of drinks into the 'extensive beer garden' who, in reality, would have been walking straight on to the busy A38 Exeter to Cullompton road!

Myrtle Devenish

Paignton's Myrtle Devenish rose to fame as the 'hang gliding granny' in the National Savings commercial! Her face should be familiar as she has been in over eighty commercials, as well as many films and television programmes. This lovable lady was the lucky one chosen out of forty hopefuls for the part for hang gliding off Milk Hill on the Marlborough Downs.

Not only did this advert help National Savings, but it also acted as a recruitment drive for potential hang glider pilots! People enlisted for courses and clubs all over Britain probably in the assumption that if a lady over seventy could do it ... The original intention was for Myrtle to fly a

A smiling Myrtle Devenish ▶

few feet above the ground but in the end she soared many times higher than this and still managed a cheery wave.

For a 'Trueprint' advert she was flown all the way to Florida and her slice of the action lasted for just a few seconds. You may have missed her if your eyes were focussed firmly on the bikini clad beauty who toppled helplessly backwards into the swimming pool – (now you remember?)

Myrtle has only been involved with some filming in Devon including *Recluse, Children of Dynmouth* and *A Winter Harvest.* She has also been in two episodes of *Coronation Street* and recorded pop songs with The Kinks. However if you are watching *Time Bandits* keep a look out for her – she is the lady wearing tea bags as earrings.

Myrtle came to Devon from South Wales at the age of ten and retains a mild Welsh accent. However, being an actress she is fully capable of other accents and was employed to work alongside Clive Gunnell to make an Ambrosia Cream Rice advert – a product 'made in Devon' with a commercial shot on what appeared to be a typical Devon farm – in Oxfordshire!

Feature Films
Made in Devon

Filming on Dartmoor

Topographically Dartmoor has much to offer the film maker, with its distant unspoilt horizons ideal for period pieces and its eye-catching scenery for the hint of romance. Its environmentally sensitive high upland moors have been used as The Klondike of North America, the Nigerian outback and even a landscape devastated by a nuclear holocaust!

Although the area is designated as a National Park, this does not mean that the National Park Authority (NPA) own the land, they merely oversee and manage it. The land ownership is greatly diversified, the Duchy of Cornwall own a large proportion, while the rest is shared between farmers, South West Water, the Forestry Commission and a variety of other landowners. Anybody wishing to make a film on Dartmoor firstly has to discover who actually owns the land on which they wish to film. Technically they do not have to get permission from the NPA, but the authority would always wish to be informed and involved for the sake of all who know and care about the moor. However, the NPA would immediately become involved if any filming was carried on at the same location for more than 28 days, as then planning permission would be officially required by the film makers.

The NPA obviously has control over its own land and exercises it with responsibility. If heavy rain has fallen for a prolonged spell, filming is not permitted as the damage caused by heavy vehicles on soft terrain can scar a landscape. There is one common on Dartmoor where the damage done by a television crew over twenty years ago can still be clearly seen. The NPA insist on all damage being made good and thereby act as a reassuring watchdog for the public's benefit. Certain sites are often in demand mainly because of accessibility. Haytor has been extensively used and the Bronze Age settlement of Grimspound is a much sought after location. The NPA try to find other similar but less sensitive areas for film companies to use.

Of the ten National Parks in England, Dartmoor would appear to be the greatest in demand by film makers as borne out by the fact that Dartmoor National Park Officer, Ian Mercer, contacted all the other parks to see how they coped with the problem, only to discover that they didn't have such a problem!

The Hound Of The Baskervilles

Just after the turn of the century, Sir Arthur Conan Doyle (1859-1930) wrote his most famous novel "The Hound of the Baskervilles". He based his story on the old Dartmoor legend about wicked Squire Richard Cabell of Buckfastleigh, who lived and died in the seventeenth century. Squire Cabell is believed to have sold his soul to the Devil and then raised hell with evil and dastardly deeds. His life's passion was hunting over the moors with his vicious pack of black hounds. On his death his body was encarcerated within a raised tomb, covered by an enormously heavy slab and surrounded by a walled building – all done to stop his wanderings beyond the grave. Yet, as in all good legends, this failed to do the trick and his baying phantom black hounds called to summon him for one last spectral hunt on a stormy night in 1677, following his funeral.

Conan Doyle was a frequent visitor to the area often staying at Park Hill House at Ipplepen and is believed to have conceived the idea for his story when visiting the Royal Duchy Hotel in Princetown – which is now the Prison Officers' Mess. He was a dedicated Spiritualist and found it hard to resist the temptation of building a story around the legend. He chose the lordly name of Baskerville from a less aristocratic root, for this was actually the name of the driver of his coach and horses who conveyed him and his friends from the moor back to Park Hill House. Baskerville Hall is probably based on Hayford Hall on the edge of the moor near Cross Furzes, the Great Grimpen Mire was based on the dreaded Foxtor Mires (a half mile wide amphitheatre of morass guaranteed to drown the spirits of any half witted creature enticed into it) and thus, born in the mists and mires of darkest Dartmoor, this tale of toil and trouble was published in 1902.

Film makers obviously couldn't resist such a dramatic tale with all the ingredients to shock and surprise an audience. Could Sherlock Holmes solve the mystery of a supernatural hound threatening the life of a Dartmoor baronet?

A 1977 British version, like the story line itself, really ended up in the mire, being described by one critic as "a pointless, pitiful and vulgar spoof of an enjoyable original." Peter Cook and Dudley Moore as Holmes and

66

Watson, respectively, were aided and abetted by a formidable cast which included Denholm Elliot, Terry Thomas, Joan Greenwood, Max Wall, Irene Handl, Kenneth Williams, Roy Kinnear, Penelope Keith, Prunella Scales and Spike Milligan.

The great popularity of Conan Doyle's work in the USA led to a remake, in 1982, especially made for American audiences. The National Trust property at Knightshayes Court near Tiverton became Baskerville Hall for the duration of the shoot. The main reason for the choice of this location was the crest of the Amory family, who formerly owned Knightshayes, being the Talbot Hound, which is to be found almost everywhere about the house. With it prominent at the fireplace, woven into the carpet of the morning room, etched onto the stained glass and even fashioned into the shaped hedges, Knightshayes seemed the perfect venue.

However, it is highly doubtful that this stately home knew what it was letting itself in for when a massive invasion of film makers moved in during November 1982. In addition to the large number of necessary personnel, all the paraphernalia needed to reconstruct sunshine, wind, rain, thunderclaps and other environmental phenomena were imported, plus all the heavy equipment, miles of cable, gantries for lights and cameras and all manner of props etc. Thus the car parks were filled to bulging in order to create a casual, elegant, set giving the overwhelming impression of a

Martin Shaw looking somewhat pensive at Knightshayes (Baskerville Hall)

quiet, turn of the century, country residence.

Even though a handsome settlement, running to a five figure fee, had been agreed with the National Trust, many other conditions had to be met and fragile items were removed from the house rather than leave them to the tender mercies of the film crew – "Take one – whoops – take two!". Almost every item removed was matched by another and there was certainly no scrimping evident. Two large Talbot hound statues were purchased but the inane grin on their faces were regarded as too stupid, and they kept falling over, so the props buyer was sent off to a Tiverton antique shop to buy two large stone dogs.

Ian Richardson played Sherlock Holmes, Donald Churchill was Dr Watson whilst Martin Shaw (*The Professionals*) played Sir Henry Baskerville. Denholm Elliot also starred in this, his second version of the famous story. Other notable actors and actresses included Eleanor Bron, Edward Judd and David Langton (Lord Bellamy of *Upstairs Downstairs*). Coincidentally there were two separate film crews – one upstairs, one downstairs!

No self respecting dramatisation of this story would have been complete without some filming shot on Dartmoor itself. Although various villages had been considered it was eventually felt that it would be better to construct a purpose built village so the ancient farmhouse at Hedge Barton, appropriately in the early morning shadow of Hound Tor, formed the

Martin Shaw (Henry Baskerville), Edward Judd (Mr Barrymore), Eleanor Bron (Mrs Barrymore) and Ian Richardson (Sherlock Holmes)

mainstay in a shrewdly constructed set. The conglomeration of farm buildings leant themselves perfectly for conversion into a village. The calves' house became a pub and, in addition to this, other outbuildings became a village shop and a police station, complete with a blue lamp, *à la Dixon of Dock Green*.

Although they were happy to go to such lengths for realism, the North Dartmoor Beagles, who were normally kennelled at Hedge Barton, had to be evacuated to a new temporary accommodation because the baying of the hounds disturbed the film makers!

Sherlock Holmes has the distinction of being the most portrayed character from fiction. Well over sixty different actors have played him including Sam Robinson, a coloured actor!

Revolution

The steady renaissance in the fortunes of the British film industry in the 1980s was dealt a considerable blow when *Revolution*, a story based on the American War of Independence (1775-1783) was released amid much publicity and fan fares only to be duly blasted by the critics. In pure financial terms the film had terrible problems and its budget of some twenty million pounds was greatly surpassed.

Although much of the film was shot in the East Anglian market town of Kings Lynn, many scenes were filmed in Devon. There were several battle scenes shot in the Burrator area of South Western Dartmoor and other sequences filmed at Kingston on the south coast of Devon.

The stars involved in the making of this dreary saga included Al Pacino, Donald Sutherland, the lovely Nastassja Kinski, Dexter Fletcher, Joan Plowright, Annie Lennox (of Eurythmics fame) and former comedian turned straight actor, Dave King. However, it was not this galaxy of stars which sent the bills rocketing skywards to an astronomical figure, but the grand scale of operations required to complete the film.

For the representation of the second battle of Upper Manhattan, filmed at Deancombe (a valley above Burrator Reservoir), between 19-21 April

The British Army in America on Dartmoor!

1985, the number of extra artistes which were employed included the following: 118 British Infantry, 50 British Light Infantry, 48 British Grenadiers, 29 British Artillery, 7 British Foot Officers, 4 British Mounted Soldiers/Officers, 10 British Drum and Fife Boys, 150 American soldiers, and 6 American Drum and Fife Boys, a staggering total of more than four hundred people.

Many of the extras were recruited from the ranks of the dole queue – a high percentage of them highly enthusiastic and active Plymouth Argyle supporters, so amidst their ranks were some notorious characters well versed in battle combat. In order to muster these men into a convincing fighting force, a genuine drill sargeant was brought in to get them into shape. He really put the men through their paces and disciplined them verbally for minor indiscretions. By the time they were ready they had acquired the necessary discipline to obey instructions without question, important because it was not possible to keep re-taking such demanding scenes as the ones in which they were involved.

The cameras rolled and the battle scenes went ahead in the smoke filled depressions above the reservoir. Many men 'died' as well as a good number of horses, but on closer inspection you may notice that the dead animals were in fact fibre glass!

A great deal of hardware was necessary. For scenes at Deancombe, a surfaced road was laid to the head of this valley. Almost an acre of steel mesh was laid down in a field, for all the vehicles to be parked without causing too much environmental damage, and along the next field a wooden railway was constructed, about eighty yards long, for a camera to be slowly moved along to film some very dramatic battle scenes.

The action was directed from the elevated hillsides by loud hailers. There is no doubt about it but the battle scenes were done so enthusiastically that a lot of people were scared out of their wits as the risk of serious injury was a real possibility.

The rifles used were the real thing and quite valuable, some reputably changed hands in back street Plymouth shops. As the days were long and occasionally hot, it became increasingly difficult to keep tabs on all the costumes and 'props'. It was known that some troops marched off the set to head for Plymouth's pubs, still fully kitted out for battle.

The preparations for the battle scenes included some quite elaborate environmental activity. The man-made structure of Burrator Dam, occasionally in camera view, was deemed to be out of keeping so, with an element of trickery, it was landscaped. A line of scaffolding and some imported vegetation eventually masked its outline.

Had the film makers had things all their own way, the major battle scenes would have been filmed near Fernworthy Reservoir, on the north eastern side of Dartmoor. They planned a massive set including a settle-

The cannons boom and the cameras roll!

ment for the area on the gentle slopes below Thornworthy Tor, but a well nurtured fear of lasting damage convinced the powers-that-be that filming should not be allowed there.

The battle of Yorktown began, for the soldiers, with an early breakfast at The Holiday Inn in Plymouth and other various hotels around that city. The 'soldiers' were then organised with military precision into four 29-seater buses and three double deckers. A minibus and twelve cars conveyed the more important members of the cast to the battlefield at Scobbiscombe Farm, Kingston on the remote coast of the South Hams, forty-five minutes being allowed for the convoy to negotiate the maze of narrow, high hedged lanes encountered after passing through Modbury en route.

A lot of ground work was done at Scobbiscombe in readiness for the battle scenes there. 'Redoubts', star shaped earthworks with a high parapet and deep trenches behind, were created, bulldozers being used to move many tons of earth.

As well as the vast cast there was all the various accoutrements of staging this mock-up of the battle of Yorktown. The props included Battle flags, Signal flags, a spyglass, a surrender flag (for the British) and a host of various weapons. For the special effects (SPFX) it was necessary to take

"Revolution"—battle scenes in Bigbury Bay

the wherewithal to produce vapours of black and white smoke, explosions, simulated canon fire and bullet hits. To restrict the amount of unneccesary casualties there was dummy tomahawks for three Hurons and two Iroquois and retractable bayonets and knives for some of the main characters. The make-up department were primed to cope with lots of blood stains and gory wounds.

The catering staff were put on standby to feed the participants, and a lull in the battle was scheduled for lunch between 11.30 – 12.30. A very necessary running buffet was provided from 18.00 – as every one knows an army marches on its stomach!

The filming at Scobbiscombe Farm was done on a number of days, the initial mass battle scenes in April 85 and the beach scenes a few weeks later. Despite the fact that the tide table was printed on the call sheets, one of the film crews on the beach had to make a fairly hasty retreat to avoid being swamped by an incoming tide that showed scant respect for the film makers! Another valuable camera, worth about £250,000, wasn't so lucky when someone pushed it over the clifftop into the sea.

The critics may have rightly accused the film of being tedious, monotonous and exceedingly dull – you only have to see it to agree – but you have to appplaud the efforts which went into creating it.

Knights Of The Round Table

Historians may argue whether or not King Arthur's 'Camelot' is in Cornwall or Somerset, but Devon can at least claim the distinction that the film *Knights of the Round Table* was made here in 1953/4. Much filming was done at Haytor where an elaborate and impressive castle was built between the two main rock piles atop the tor.

From 'Camelot' at Haytor, a fine view presents itself over South Devon. In the distance the Teign Estuary can be spied with the Ness, a great Sandstone cliff, standing sentinel at its mouth. Here 'Arthur' tried to throw Excalibur into the water, only to have the scene completely ruined by a passing aeroplane overhead!

Along with Stanley Baker was Mel Ferrer as King Arthur, Robert Taylor as Lancelot and Ava Gardner as Guinevere, an actress once voted as the most beautiful woman in the world! It took a long time to incorporate Haytor's twin masses into an Arthurian setting but once created it made a striking backcloth of action for spectators to watch, from a distance, with many traditional medieval sports being staged for the film, jousting being the most spectacular.

Lancelot's efforts to defeat the evil Modred were not altogether appreciated by the film critics who described it as 'disappointingly flat' which makes rather a nice contrast with Dartmoor itself!

Run Wild, Run Free

In 1969 David Rook's novel "The White Colt" was made into a film called *Run Wild, Run Free*. John Mills, Sylvia Sims, Bernard Miles, Gordon Jackson, a young Fiona Fullerton and even younger Mark Lester all came to Dartmoor to tell this story of a mute boy struggling to regain his self confidence, and ultimately his voice, through his relationship with one special animal. Newton Abbot was used as the unnamed market town for several shots to help complete a slow moving but atmospheric tale with a happy ending.

However, that happy ending nearly didn't happen. Anyone who has seen the film will recall the most dramatic final scenes where everybody struggles against the odds to extricate the colt from a moorland bog. With great difficulty, much exhaustion and, eventually, tears of relief and joy the pony is freed and the boy speaks for the first time.

Initially an artificial bog was constructed but it did not look authentic enough so it was decided to use the real thing, an event which was planned to last ten to fifteen minutes. On a day which was cold, misty and dark,

'Snowball' a Welsh Mountain pony, was covered in many layers of grease to give her some protection against the harsh cold and penetrating moisture of the mire. But the mire was much deeper than anticipated and it was soon realised that Snowball was genuinely stuck and in real danger. If the acting appeared convincing it was because the situation was real, and the only way the pony could be extricated, after much genuine anguish, was with a great deal of skill and patience – to the great relief of all concerned.

Shivering and distressed Snowball spluttered from the dire mire to be immediately engulfed with the milk of human kindness, actually she was drenched with brandy to help revive her. It took a year or more for her to fully recover but the story has a happy ending. At the time of writing, many years on since the film, Snowball survives as a very fit thirty-five year old with hardly any ailments to trouble her and no signs of arthritic problems.

The Apple Tree

Kitty Jay was a young serving girl who fell in love with someone above her station. When she became pregnant and had no one to turn to, she hung herself in a barn. Being a suicide victim her body was buried at the nearest crossroads and, to this day, fresh flowers are always on her grave.

Celebrated playwright John Galsworthy had very strong connections with Devon; for many years he lived at Manaton on Dartmoor. It is quite likely that it was on one of his walking jaunts to the other side of Hayne Down that he heard the story of Kitty Jay and found his inspiration for a short story, written in 1916, called "The Apple Tree" which contained enough passion and drama to merit dramatisation.

Galsworthy's story, set in the halcyon days of 1902, features a newly qualified barrister called Ashton (James Wilby) who has been on a walking tour of Dartmoor. Unfortunately the young man falls foul of the rocky terrain on the moor and twists his ankle. The injury forces him to spend time in a remote Dartmoor farmhouse where Mrs Narracombe (Susannah York) takes care of him. Whilst recovering Ashton falls madly in love with Mrs. Narracombe's niece, a beautiful young girl called Megan (Imogen Stubbs) and they start a strong, passionate and illicit love affair – the sort of literary recipe guaranteed to please millions of viewers.

As this was set in the days before push button money machines, Ashton has to go to Torquay to have money sent down to him, to fund his elopement with Megan. Almost immediately he bumps into an old school friend who is holidaying with his three sisters, the oldest being sophisticated, elegant and beautiful, a prime candidate for further romance. He is

This is Torquay in the story but Sidmouth in real life—the perfect picture to show how a screen set can be so convincing

persuaded to stay with them and gets caught up again in his real world of privilege and refinement. Meanwhile, back on the remote moorland farm Megan becomes impatient and eventually comes looking for Ashton ...

As Torquay has lost much of its regency elegance, particularly on the seafront, the film company had no hesitation in using Sidmouth. Sidmouth is an ideal resort for period pieces as, unlike most other seaside towns, it does not boast a surfeit of bingo halls, neon signs, or modern buildings. It is quiet and sedate, like most watering places used to be, and can be easily adapted for costume dramas. However film crews are not always welcome additions and some residents were upset that they couldn't use their favourite part of the beach, or because of the restricted access to several roads, and a local trader complained bitterly that his delivery lorry was delayed for a considerable time. The materials laid down in the road also created a nuisance as residents were annoyed by the dust and dirt which was kicked up. And perhaps the most dreadful of all the intrusions into the normally peaceful setting of sleepy Sidmouth was that some croquet games were delayed!

Local windsurfers had to be watched to ensure they remained out of the frame as three crabbers and a ninety-year-old fishing ketch, out of

Dartmouth, sailed across the bay as a backcloth to the filming. Fishermen mended their nets and swimmers clad in gaily striped costumes populated the beach. The seafront or Esplanade was awash with fine Victorian ladies and upstanding Victorian gentlemen.

Two hundred 'extras' were employed and these were bussed in from Exeter each day. The older ladies who were sporting modern hairstyles could conceal their hair with elaborate hats, but the men had to be given extremely short Victorian haircuts which, considering the hot weather during filming, was much appreciated. Despite the intense heat no complaints were heard from the ladies wearing heavy silk and lace dresses, even though some were wearing corsets for the first time ever.

The little tots dressed in their tiny sailor hats and tiny boaters looked as cute today as they did some eighty years ago. One of these little sailor boys had the on screen task of consuming an ice cream in a scene which featured Megan. To the child's delight, there were ten 'takes' before the director was satisfied.

The Exeter Railway Band also had to don uniforms of the Army variety and, as it turned out, it was more like Dad's Army. Many members of the Railway Band were on railway duty and so their retired senior members stood in and proved to be just the ticket, one of them being over eighty years old and he made it to the end of the prom.

Sidmouth's very own John Smith ready for action

Holiday makers who observed the set were thoroughly taken with it all and the film crew observed that more footage of film was probably shot by the visitors than by themselves!

A 'bank' was constructed at Sidmouth, but had to be transported to Bayard's Cove, Dartmouth for filming. It was only a frontage held up by scaffolding but looked so convincing that several visitors were thwarted in their efforts to cash a cheque. Dartmouth's job centre, in Higher Street, changed its colours for a day and became Torquay Post Office, whilst another old antique shop was converted into a drapers store. Other well known locations used included Cricket St Thomas where *To the Manor Born* was filmed, the Italian Gardens and the Palm House at Bicton Park in East Devon.

"The Apple Tree" at Sidmouth (Torquay)

For the farmhouse scenes, a remote stone farmhouse on Exmoor had its slate roof covered in deep thatch and a new/old porch was added. Another farm, this time genuinely on Dartmoor, also hosted the annual sheep-shearing party, but a flock of Cheviot sheep had to considerably agree to retain their fleeces a few extra weeks longer than usual so that they could make their film debuts whilst a sheepshearing sequence was successfully shot (try saying that fast!).

The Stick Up (Mud)

At the peak of his popularity, David Soul (real name David Solberg) visited Devon to make a film which was beset with problems from start to finish and beyond! Earning the quote, "The worst film of this or possibly any year" from Barry Took in Punch, The Stick Up (also known as *Mud*) was shot entirely on location on the western flanks of Dartmoor in 1977.

Although most people will recall this as the second year of the 1976/77 drought, the film makers managed to choose a period which was wild, wet and windy. In a scene where David Soul had to ride a motor cycle through a wooden hut, it needed so many takes that by the time it was 'in the can' he was soaked to the bone. His response to the regular drenchings was to publically strip down to his briefs!

On another similar occasion when the star actor stripped to a state of semi-nudity, he grabbed the tail of a passing cow and, in a fashion resembling a waterskiier, was pulled across the field, skidding over many a cow pat fresh or otherwise.

It might well have been his bravado in the face of adversity, and in the face of an unrelenting southwesterly, that contributed to the 'poor Soul' catching pneumonia.

This comedy thriller set in Devon in 1935, used locations at Yelverton, Milton Combe, Tavistock and Merrivale. Wherever the crew went David Soul was the target of exceedingly enthusiastic girl fans. He was so harrassed by hordes of admiring females that he beat a hasty retreat from the limelight at every conceivable opportunity but his body guards saw to it that his heavily veiled caravan was a sanctuary.

His enforced exile, whilst recuperating from his bout of pneumonia, posed problems and it wasn't until June that he was well enough to make the concluding bits of the film. According to the monthly "The Starsky and Hutch Magazine", Volume 8, it was a mad scramble for David Soul to record the last few scenes before heading back to the United States to record more episodes of *Starsky and Hutch*.

The film was regarded as a 'low budget' venture but this of course is relative, as to most of us a similar outlay would represent a fortune. A fairground was set up with its Golden Gallopers and Big Wheel. One of the extras was stuck up at the top of it so long, again fully exposed to a roaring wind and lashing rain, that she became hysterical and another of her colleagues had to sing to her to calm her down.

A particularly spectacular mud brawl was staged in the Big Top arena. To add to the atmosphere the paid spectators were urged to sing "Mud Glorious Mud" with great gusto. But beyond the filming things got a little out of hand and some hefty sailors from Devonport, employed as extras for the day, threw some girls into the ring and then added the film director for good measure. At the end of all the revelry all one could see of any of the participants were the whites of their eyes. With a touch of irony, while the whole site outside was awash with mud, the massive mud bath inside had to be created!

The £10 a day that the extras were paid for their twelve-hour stints was obviously hard earned.

Hilda Downey, an extra moonlighting from her normal occupation as a nurse, spent the long waits between scenes reading palms. She told one lady that her daughter would become famous and sure enough, from the obscurity of a moorland edge background, Caroline Seaward became a beauty queen, a 'James Bond girl', and an ex-girlfriend of Prince Andrew.

A pumping station near Yelverton, belonging to the local water authority, with the aid of a life size facade, was converted into a 1930s petrol station. The mock-up was obviously convincing as many a motorist couldn't understand why they were unable to fill up!

David Soul is known to have enjoyed his filming in Devon, despite the vagaries of the weather, and despite being refused entry to the Riverside Club in Exeter because he was wearing jeans. The extras who worked with him were full of praise for his spirited attempts to produce an entertaining and funny film. Unfortunately *The Stick Up* was a dismal failure and it was not given a general release, but the extras and their relations did get to see it once at a special showing in Plymouth.

Cottage on Dartmoor

A variation on the theme of the eternal triangle provided the plot for this film made on Dartmoor. It was one of the earliest talkies made and starred Norah Baring, Uno Hemming, Hans Schlettow and Judd Green. The plot involved a Dartmoor farmer's wife who harbours an 'on the run' escapee from H M Prison. It also happens to be that he is an ex-lover of the said farmer's wife. Made in 1929 it was shot in black and white, and was an early forerunner of a whole spate of 'prison' movies which followed over the next decade – mostly set in American prisons.

Suspicion

When a rather sedate young lady who inherits money from her father, weds an irresponsible and penniless playboy, a situation develops into one of immense Suspicion, does he love her or does he want to murder her? HTV did a remake of the 1941 Alfred Hitchcock movie (which starred Joan Fontaine and Cary Grant), Jane Curtain and Anthony Andrews taking the starring roles for HTV's interpretation of the story. British Rail Western Region allowed the use of a coach from the VSOE, Minerva which formed with Mk I BR Stock to recreate the 1950s. The train ran from Bristol to Exeter via Reading but the photograph was taken at Castle Cary where the crew stopped for lunch.

▶

Jane Curtain and Anthony Andrews apparently on the Orient Express but strangely running through Devon!

The Ghost Train

When the moon is right a phantom locomotive plies the railway line between Dawlish Warren and Teignmouth, thundering through the wave battered stations on an unknown journey ...

It was that grand old man, Arnold Ridley, better known as Private Godfrey in *Dad's Army*, who wrote the play *The Ghost Train*. It has been filmed three times, first in 1927 as a silent movie and a second version was made in 1931. In the third film made in 1941, several scenes were shot along this unique stretch of the Devon coastline, although Cornwall was the setting in the play. This last film starred Arthur Askey and amongst his 'playmates' were Richard Murdoch and Kathleen Harrison.

Press For Time

Norman Wisdom, the British slapstick comedian, known for his doleful looks and down and out expressions, was born in 1918 and also in 1920, depending on which reference source you prefer to accept. One fact though

which is indisputable, having been researched personally, is that he came to Teignmouth in 1966 for a film called *Press for Time*.

In return for the disruption the filming was bound to cause, the local council cannily negotiated an agreement that the name of the town was to be used. However, a slight change (in spelling only) was acceptable, and so the sign at the station was amended to 'Tinmouth'. Most of the filming was completed at the station or around the sea front, the most elaborate stunt involving a bus which ran down Ivy Lane and into the Teign (or is it the Tin?) estuary.

With the co-operation of the local police force, the bus was due to run away down a narrow 1 in 6 hill, go across the sea front, over the Den, descend Ivy Lane to end up in the estuary. It is perhaps comforting to know that it wasn't quite as straightforward as that and, before an acceptable 'take' was in the can, the bus constantly stopped short, getting bogged down in soft sand many yards short of its intended location.

A few scenes were shot at a private bungalow in Shaldon, one of the few homes large enough to accommodate a film crew and all the necessary paraphernalia. An eye witness to the proceedings informed us that there

Norman Wisdom with some eager autograph hunters at the Royal Hotel in Teignmouth

was indeed much merrymaking to spice up the hum drum humour of the film script. Norman Wisdom maintained a most professional profile and really applied himself to the task in hand. Observers were greatly impressed by his efforts to inject life into a film which was not particularly well received. It appears that this diminutive man was able to mix with all types and ages of person and was literally the life and soul of the party.

On one of the evenings away from filming he attended a reception to raise funds for a local charity. He auctioned a bottle of champagne for £120 which, in 1966, was quite a 'staggering' amount.

The System

In Britain it was called *The System*, but a less subtle, though perhaps more apt and explanatory, title was used in America, *The Girl Getters*.

Oliver Reed, Jane Merrow, Barbara Ferris, Julia Foster, David Hemmings, John Alderton, Andrew Ray, Derek Nimmo and Harry Andrews were all involved in this film which was shot almost entirely in Torbay. Michael Winner, who has directed many entertaining films, worked on this story about a group of seaside layabouts who evolved a system for dating girl visitors to the mythical seaside resort of Roxham.

The arch schemer, a photographer named Tinker, portrayed by Oliver Reed, sent his comrades to join an incoming train at a stop further up the line. These 'spies' would scour the length of the train and note all the likely 'talent'. On arrival in Torquay, sorry Roxham, this information was passed to Tinker who would quickly snap a souvenir photo of each girl and collect their names and addresses where they were staying (in order to deliver the picture). This eliminated the usual chance factor in bumping into the right girls before too much of their holiday stay was wasted.

Unfortunately things start to go wrong when Tinker uncharacteristically falls for a classier-than-usual girl who doesn't fit easily into the "love 'em and leave 'em system", which then starts to break down.

There were many locations used in the Torbay area and close scrutiny will reveal the Palm Court Hotel, Torquay Sea Front and station, Livermead Beach and Paignton Pier all as they were in 1964 when the film was shot.

Mrs Stokes of Torquay was employed as an extra for a wedding reception scene. The young assistant director was so taken with her white hat and its frilly bow he placed her in a strategic position, holding a glass of champagne to toast the happy couple. Feeling that her outfit would be made complete by one of the many carnations being handed out to the 'guests', she timidly asked for one, only to be shot down by the reply,

"Don't worry darling, we're only shooting you from behind so you won't need one."

Described by one critic as "A modest, skilful, charming and fairly dishonest little picture", the book of the film described itself as a novel of "cynical sex and flaring violence – story of seaside kicks and sudden disillusion – a story of to-day"!

That Summer!

This film, which was almost entirely shot on location in Torquay, was a relatively low budget effort and, like *The System*, was another story of teenage strife and love in a seaside resort.

The 'plot' follows two girls who resign from their dull factory jobs in Leeds to spend a summer in Torquay working as chambermaids in a plush hotel. Although the resort is frequently referred to, the Imperial Hotel where they were employed was not named. They meet up with two teen-age lads, one straight from Borstal but, after showing his tough side, we see a better side emerge, which is just as well because at the end of the film we have to cheer him on in a swimming race. The fourth one is more or less included just to make up the foursome.

Many of Torquay's attractions appear in the film. The Amusement Arcade introduces us to the opposition, a nasty teenage trio from the North. They then turn up at such regular intervals at the same venues as the 'good guys' that we are given the impression that Torquay is so small you get to know all the visitors personally!

The fictional 'Devon Swimming Race' is the climax of the film, an event which involved swimming from Meadfoot Beach and out around the Bay before returning to the start. Our young 'hero' practises hard, with great devotion, even to the point of falling out with his girl friend, whilst his main rival, one of the terrible trio, indulges in a spate of drugs, boozing, bullying and general nastiness. It would appear he shouldn't stand a chance in such a fitness event but is, incredibly, a very tough opponent. However, on race day, our hero starts 200 yards behind the other competitors, fights the baddy, extracts a confession in front of the police, and then races off to overtake everyone else and win the race. Hooray!

Isadora

Isadora Duncan was an exciting but eccentric American dancer whose inspiration came from ancient Greek art. She was an advocate of freedom

Oldway Mansion in Paignton, star of so many films

of movement and expression, which she displayed in her lifestyle.

In 1909 Isadora came to Devon as a guest of Paris Singer of Oldway Mansion at Paignton. She was thirty-one years old at the time and fell in love with her host. Love supposedly blossomed during the long and wet summer and free expression is believed to have been employed behind a screen in the ballroom on a wet and windy afternoon. At her disposal was a fleet of fourteen automobiles and a yacht. She met her untimely death in 1927 when her scarf became entangled in the wheel of her open top car.

In 1968 Universal made a lavish film of her life. For this biopic seventy-two locations were used with filming also in Yugoslavia, Italy and France. It was appropriate that Oldway should be used even though it had ceased to be a residence and had become council offices. The film starred Vanessa Redgrave with Jason Robards Jnr as Paris Singer.

Although the classic appearance of Oldway had not changed greatly it was deemed necessary to add some extra touches. Enormous polystyrene statues were brought in – these were so light that staff could easily carry a statue under each arm. However their lack of substance caused problems whenever there was a gust of wind because they kept blowing over. Eventually vandals got at them and disfigured their anatomies beyond repair.

Some musicians employed on the set had to perform under very difficult circumstances; they were harnessed and left to hang or dangle from the exceedingly high, ornate ceiling whilst they accompanied Isadora. Fortunately the rate of pay was regarded as extremely generous. This was collected, at the end of each session, in cash from a small booth. The paymaster never appeared to look up and it was felt that almost anyone could just mutter a name to be handed an envelope packed with crisp bank notes.

Carpenters on the set were required to mask two arches which led to the public conveniences. This they did expertly so that a distant view of public urinals did not take the classic edge off Isadora's dancing. The timber and boards used in 1968 still lie (at the time of writing) propped up against the walls of the tennis changing rooms.

What cinemagoers rarely see. Filming at Oldway

The French Lieutenant's Woman

Lyme Regis lies on the 'wrong' side of the Devon/Dorset border by just a few hundred yard and, as we are sticklers for detail, we unfortunately cannot include some of the wonderful stories surrounding this much revered royal seaside resort. One of the principal films made on location in this part of the world was a Harold Pinter interpretation of John Fowles' book, *The French Lieutenant's Woman*, a highly acclaimed film.

Fortunately for us the film crew got their passports together and entered Devon to do some shooting at Exeter. However, the 'Exeter' in the film was in fact Kingswear, opposite Dartmouth. The reason why the genuine article was not used was that the film, set in the year 1867, required arrival at Exeter station by steam train, and who other than the Torbay and South Devon Railway could provide such a service?

Jeremy Irons, Meryl Streep and Leo McKern were the main stars in this epic film which serenely glided across the screens for over two hours. Unfortunately the filming of some of the sequences at Kingswear did not run in the same smooth fashion. A train arriving at 'Exeter' had to arrive no less than fourteen times before they got it right. Even British Rail doesn't usually need that many attempts to arrive on time!

Filming this scene and others here was done over two days. On the first day it poured with rain but on the second day the weather was fine. In order to maintain continuity the platforms had to be soaked by hoses and manufactured smoke was created to block out the bright daylight.

Great trouble was taken to whisk Kingswear back to 1867. For shots taken on the hill up to the Steam Packet Inn rubber cobble stones were installed along the edge of Fore Street, whilst the road markings were masked by other materials. Almost all the buildings were repainted, the Royal Dart being painted brown and cream, the colours of the Great Western Railway. A safety wall running down the estuary side of the street was coated in plaster of paris and several false lamp posts were located. A Victorian stall was set up selling fish and, as plastic fish were just not convincing enough, real ones had to be used for authenticity.

Daily life in Kingswear was disrupted considerably for a short time whilst the extensive preparations and film shooting took place. The lower car ferry was stopped for the day so that crowd and market scenes would be filmed without interruption. But at least The Steam Packet, where bar and bedroom scenes were filmed, escaped without too much upheaval.

The plot or story line of this film about making a film, involved the key characters paralleling the film characters they portrayed. Set in 1867 a Victorian gentleman forsakes his fiancée for the charm and dark mystery of the abandoned mistress of a French seaman (Goodbye Sailor?). The film itself was rather muddled, constantly switching back and forth, and the critics generally agreed that whilst there were some lovely moments magically portrayed, the overall impression was that it was like watching an animated museum piece set in a glass case cocooned from reality.

The Sailor Who Fell From Grace With The Sea

This is not the sort of film title which rolls smoothly off the tongue, nor does it lend itself to easy instant recall. Not of course that anyone would want to remember this film when the very nature of it produced responses like this from the critics ...

"This everyday tale of torture scopophilia, copulation, masturbation, dismemberment and antique dealing deserves to be traded back to the Japs and made required viewing for timorous kamikazi pilots" so wrote Benny Green in "Punch".

And where did all these fun and games take place? Dartmouth, dear old lovable Dartmouth, as respectable a place as you could ever expect to find until Sarah Miles, Kris Kristofferson, Earl Rhodes, Jonathan Kahn, Marge Cunningham and co, acted out this sorry tale in which a precocious boy jeopardised his widowed mother's chances of a romance with a sailor by castrating him.

Despite the awful revues from the critics and the hot reception from many shocked Dartmouth townspeople, there were a few minor compensations. Most people agreed that the camera crew shot some wonderful background scenes of the town and its surroundings and, in conjunction with the use of Dartmouth's real name, this might have persuaded many newcomers to visit such a lovely area.

Kris Kristofferson became a popular celebrity with the local population and turned up at the folk club held at the Seal Arms in Dartmouth, although some 'finger in the ear' traditionalists were not over enthusiastic about his choice of song or his impersonation of Leonard Cohen.

The Lonely Road

Clive Brook and Victoria Hopper were two great stars who had long careers and were well established by the 1930s. It was then they came to Devon, Dartmouth in particular, to make *The Lonely Road*. The theme of the film involved many smuggling scenes and Blackpool Sands was chosen for night filming, using large arc lights to illuminate the scene.

The entire crew stayed at The Raleigh Hotel in Dartmouth and used it as their base for filming all around the district. St Petrox Church at Dartmouth Castle was used for a screen wedding and a lovely local girl called Jean Trowson was picked to be the movie 'bride'.

Bequest To The Nation

This is the story of Lord Nelson's enduring love affair with Lady Hamilton, a story of romance and adventure. Playwright Terence Rattigan had a 'good eye' for such a story and penned the play on which the film was based. In the USA it was called *The Nelson Affair* which, considering the year in which it was set, has rather a modern ring to it. The beginning and end sequences of the film, which involved such stars as Peter Finch, Glenda Jackson, Anthony Quayle and Nigel Stock, were made at Dartmouth.

Dartmouth was chosen because of its maritime traditions and its lovely setting. There is also the obvious need for the extras to be well versed in maritime skills, and what better place to find an army (or should it be navy?) of extras able to cope with the demands of endless rowing and hopping in and out of boats with practised ease? Also the expertise of cadets from Britannia Royal Naval College, in the appropriate costume of the day, was utilised on several occasions.

However, Dartmouth's huge popularity with the yachting fraternity created some problems – there were simply too many modern yachts in the background. Ever resourceful, the film crew assembled a large glass screen with cut-outs of old fashioned luggers pasted on and, hey presto! the instant camouflage also provided the perfect backcloth.

Ordeal By Innocence

A film Made in Devon during February/March with scenes of constant lashing rain and all-veiling mists sounds just about right ... Unfortunately, in the making of *Ordeal By Innocence*, Devon's normal, inclement meteorological elements must have taken a holiday, for it was left to the 'special effects' team to artificially create wet streets, wet car windscreens and on some occasions, wet actors. The film was shot on location in the South Hams in 1984. The days of filming at Dartmouth were generally long and tiring ones for the entire crew. A scene in the wet, but filmed whilst dry, demanded many takes over quite a considerable period of time. Every so often somebody had to go around with a watering can and sprinkle the actors!

Several locations in Dartmouth were used which included the Royal Castle Hotel, the Old Fire Station, the passenger ferry quay, and the Dart Marina Hotel. Just upstream several scenes were shot at Greenway Quay and at Maypool. Other important locations included Totnes, Kingsbridge, Paignton and Widdecombe House at Stokenham.

Donald Sutherland on a South Devon beach

A glittering array of stars and well known actors were assembled to interpret the screenplay of yet another dramatised Agatha Christie story, shot in an area where she lived for many years. Canadian actor Donald Sutherland, who starred in this film was only one year old when the first Agatha Christie story was made into a film in 1936. He was joined by Sarah Miles, Valerie Whittington, Ian McShane, Diana Quicke, Annette Crosbie, Faye Dunaway, Michael Elphick, Brian Glover and a whoopee cushion who all combined to make a happy team for the six weeks it took to make this film.

In the film a doctor of geology (Donald Sutherland) gives a man a lift in his car whilst on his way to a port, heading for the Antarctic for four years of research. Having discovered his passenger's wallet, he attempts to return it when he returns to England four years later. In the ensuing four years the poor passenger has been wrongly accused of murder and his alibi, in the Antarctic, couldn't be traced. The doctor decides to investigate.

Dave 'Spud' Murphy was a most useful source of information about *Revolution* and also *Ordeal By Innocence*. The common denominator between these two films was Donald Sutherland. As Spud was of the same height, colouring and physique he was used as his stand-in for both these films. At a height of over six feet tall, there are not that many suitable substitutes available for Donald Sutherland. A stand-in's role is to go through the actor's paces on set for him whilst the film technicians plot each camera angle and scene with meticulous accuracy. On one occasion the stand-in had a stand-in – the actor! When Mr Sutherland realised that poor Spud had been working solidly with no break, he offered to take his place while Spud went off for some breakfast. On another occasion Spud turned up for what he thought was going to be indoor shots. Alas the poor fellow was taken into a muddy field, clad only in light indoor shoes. When the gallant Mr Sutherland arrived and saw his predicament the star actor immediately sent for some of his own personal ski boots which Spud used for the following days.

Obviously a likeable character, the concentration of those on set was occasionally sorely tested by Donald Sutherland who, despite his highly professional approach to film making, liked to play pranks on the others. With his actor's perfect timing he carefully picked his moments to strategically locate his whoopee cushion, reducing everybody to hysterics. In a serious scene with Michael Elphick, who was the Police Inspector, they left the house where the murdered body lay, and got into a Riley. As Mr Elphick sat himself down in the rear of the car, the most horrendous sounding raspberry was broadcast loud and clear!

The film crew played its own elaborate prank, albeit unintentional, at the expense of a member of the public this time. In the screenplay a Point to Point race meeting was to be held. For practical reasons a real life Point to Point at Bowden Pillers, near Totnes, was used. In a corner of a distant field a set was constructed with all the normal paraphernalia associated with such affairs of the Turf. To create an authentic scene the props de-

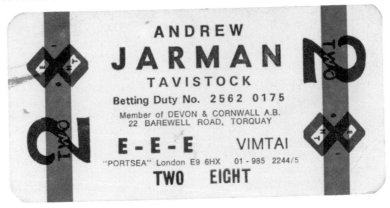

partment went to the trouble of printing fake ten shilling notes and racing cards like the one shown in the picture. To animate the scene a merry band of bona fide Bookmakers set up shop while fifteen lady and twenty gentlemen punters mulled around, all appropriately attired in 1950s dress, the period of the film.

Now deep in the rural heart of the South Hams, fashion tends to lay a little behind the times – in this case about thirty years! One South Hams farmer, bedecked in clothing from the same bygone days as the rest of the company, saw nothing unusual in the set up whatsoever. Blissfully unaware of his intrusion, he mingled with the extras. He didn't even suspect there was something peculiar going on when he consulted his race card and couldn't find any of the names on his list to match those on the starting board, or on the bookmakers' chalk boards. Undaunted he approached to place a bet for £1. The crew played along with the charade for a short while before coming clean. As he ambled away, they heard him mutter, "Cor b***** me"!

One's sympathies go out to the continuity person who had to keep tracks of the 'dead body' discovered in the sheds of the Dart Marina Hotel. As the filming straddled the lunch hour, the corpse duly got up, ate a hearty meal (which no doubt filled a little hole), and then went back to being 'dead'.

Torbay Cinema is one of the grandest small picture houses in the West of England. Internally it is a masterpiece of local craftsmanship, constructed in 1913, a time when the mega cinema was unknown in this part of the world. The individuality of this emporium of entertainment made it an ideal location for scene 59 of *Ordeal*. The upstairs, or balcony, scene featured Donald Sutherland, Cassie Stewart and an usherette with only two rows of seats being left intact, the others having been removed for the cameras to glide around without unnecessary obstacles. Thirty five extras were strategically located downstairs, and for the air of reality a smoke machine was used to give the atmosphere that cigarette smoke laden look. John Mann, the cinema's projectionist, had the disarming experience of showing this film in his cinema. Imagine him looking at people sat in the cinema watching the film of people sat in the cinema watching the film ...

Ironically, whilst the interior was perfect, the exterior of the Torbay Cinema failed to meet requirements so the outside of The Royalist at Dartmouth (since demolished) was substituted.

A large country house called Argyle Point was featured in the story. Its equivalent in film locations were Widdecombe House, between Stokenham and Beesands, and Stokenham House nearby. Again the majority of the internal shots were of Widdecombe House, the external ones being of Stokenham House. It was decided on one fine, beautiful morning

Donald Sutherland and Annette Crosbie during a lunchbreak from "Ordeal by Innocence"

to shoot some outside scenes here. However, a man on a hang glider, curious about the proceedings going on hundreds of feet below, swooped down to inspect. As he was in camera shot the director got extremely upset and excessive use of flagellating arms and a loud hailer resulted in the poor fellow making a hasty retreat on the thermals.

At Widdecombe House the lodge and gates were also used. Extras in the film were completely taken in by the impressively ornate gates which they assumed were genuine. Their suspicions were aroused when they realised how easily they swung in the breeze and, on closer inspection, they turned out to be wooden!

The end of filming was celebrated with a darts match and party in Dartmouth, and Donald Sutherland presented several specially inscribed and autographed silver tankards to those who worked with him. This is now one of 'Spud' Murphy's most treasured possessions.

The Supergrass

The Supergrass was one of the few films encountered in the research of this book which used the actual place names of the places featured in the film. This was a production attributed to the 'Comic Strip' team who did several short comedy films for Channel 4 mentioned elsewhere in this book. The team in this film included the regulars and several guest stars – Dawn French, Jennifer Saunders, Adrian Edmonson, Robbie Coltraine, Nigel Planer, Peter Richardson, Alexei Sayle, Keith Allen, Ronald Allen and Michael Elphick.

Billed as a 'comedy thriller', this was a "tale of Sex, Drugs, Cream Teas and Murder by the Seaside", centering on a drugs racket called 'Operation Bolt Head', an appropriate code name as most of the action took place at Hope Cove near Bolt Head.

Several scenes were shot on Dartmoor and the standard distortion of truth took place with sequences at the Warren House, Widecombe, Poundsgate, Cold East Cross and Hexworthy all neatly edited together to give the stars a smooth drive across the moor, rather than an irrational hopping about to a combination of unrelated places

The final scenes of the film showed a van, with drugs supposedly stowed away on board, escaping towards Haytor. The sequence has been edited in such a fashion that with each clip they are further back down the road on which they have just driven along. Drugs can indeed have an amazing effect on things!

Catch Us If You Can

The song "Catch us if your can" was probably more memorable than the film of the same title. In America the film had the alternative title *Having a Wild Weekend*, and was a lively portrayal of a group of stuntmen having many adventures in South West England. It was made in 1965 when it was in vogue for young pop groups to make high spirited youthful films featuring themselves. In this case the Dave Clark Five clowned around in much the same way as the Beatles did before them and a little like the Monkees did after them on TV. They were aided and abetted by Barbara Ferris, Robin Bailey and the late Yootha Joyce, and much of the filming was done at Bigbury in South Devon.

Holocaust 2000

This was not a sequel to Grecian 2000 but watching this over elaborate, pseudo intellectual film might well make you turn prematurely grey!

In this film a scene was shot at Burgh Island, off the South Devon coast at Bigbury-on-Sea. Chosen for its geographical phenomenum of an incoming tide approaching from two opposite sides across a sandy causeway, this beautiful bay was the ideal spot for a dramatic and sinister moment.

Starring Kirk Douglas and Simon Ward, the film was a GB/Italian production made in 1977. It involved the boss of a Middle East thermonuclear plant getting involved with an evil legend. He tracked down an ageing scientist who had been in hiding and met him on the sands between the island and the shore. The wise old scientist warned him that if he persisted with his plans of thermonuclear energy, all manner of dire consequences would happen. As the dialogue became more heated the burning passion of the conversation was swamped by the incoming tide which, once started, rushed in at speed and almost consumed Kirk Douglas. He frantically raced to the shore splashing through the ever deepening water and reached safety just in time. Looking back, his companion was gone ...

The best way to describe it is that it was a bit like Moses parting the Red Sea in reverse – But unlike a special effect created in a studio, the opportunities for re-taking this scene were minimal – just imagine the scene – "Thank you everyone, that was terrific – did you get that Camera One? The lens cap? What do you mean you forgot to take off the lens cap?"

International Velvet

One of the few things *International Velvet* would appear to have in common with its superior predecessor, *National Velvet*, is that its running time of 125 minutes is the same! Intended as a sequel to the Elizabeth Taylor 'classic', Brian Forbes both wrote it and directed it, and cast his wife, Nanette Newman, in the role of the grown up Velvet Brown. The original film showed how young Velvet trained and rode her horse, The Pie, to victory in the Grand National; in the sequel The Pie's son, Arizona Pie, is trained for the Olympic Three Day Event of dressage, cross-country and showjumping.

The American influence is strong, Tatum O'Neal (Ryan's daughter) arrives from Arizona as a beligerant orphan, who is taken in by her well heeled Aunt Velvet and her live-in lover (played by Canadian Christopher Plummer). After she has ridden to victory for the British Olympic team, she falls into the arms of her American boyfriend. With some excrutiating line to speak, much of the dialogue is stilted but Anthony Hopkins, in his role as selector/manager of the British team, manages to add a touch of class to a film which can have little appeal, other than to horse lovers.

Many counties in England were used for location filming, Lancashire and Lincolnshire, Buckinghamshire and Berkshire, and Warwickshire and Essex were all featured. The Devonshire connection lies at the Flete Estate deep in the South Hams of Devon.

Mothecombe Beach appears in both the opening and closing sequences and is much in evidence in between. In the opening shots and titles aerial photography lead us across the cliffs skirting Bigbury Bay and over Scobbiscombe (where *Revolution* met its Waterloo – or its Yorktown!). In the closing sequence, a long list of credits gives us more time to appreciate the aerial shots of the lovely mouth of the Erme and Mothecombe Beach. A close inspection of the last few frames will also reveal the distant white mountains of china clay spoil heaps thrown up at Lee Moor, on the south western side of Dartmoor. (Lee Moor is of course the village and not the character Lee played by a young Chris Quentin who might well be spotted by *Coronation Street* buffs.)

I Live In Grosvenor Square

During the Second World War the Americans took over a considerable area of land in the South Hams in order to rehearse for the invasion of Normany on D-Day. The local inhabitants of several villages were given about six weeks warning and were obliged to evacuate the area completely. This resulted in seven parishes, nearly two hundred farms, and a total of three thousand people being affected. Life was severely disrupted, some people even commited suicide and many homes were destroyed. Such dire consequences produced much public dismay and so a film was created in 1945 which spelt out to the Americans what chaos and strife occurred in South Devon. The film was called *I Live in Grosvenor Square* and starred Rex Harrison, Robert Morley, Dean Jagger, Dame Irene Vanbrugh (who was born in Exeter at Heavitree Vicarage in December 1872) and Anna Neagle. It was directed by Miss Neagle's husband, Herbert Wilcox.

The American title of this film was *A Yank in London*, and was the story of a duke's daughter who falls in love with a sergeant from the US Airforce.

Totnes featured heavily in this film, and many of the locals were used as incidental extras. One group of curious spectators, sitting on the church wall near the Guildhall, waited patiently to see a scene filmed involving the stars. They were disappointed when filming was stopped because of the adverse weather conditions, but just as they were about to leave, the director rushed up and asked them if they could all come back for the next three days – and be handsomely paid for the privilege. Apparently they had been captured on film as part of the crowd who were sorely disappointed that the Rex Harrison character had failed to be elected, and for the sake of continuity they were needed to be seen sitting on the same wall when filming restarted!

Another local man, John Finch, who may be remembered as the custodian of Totnes Castle for many years, was famed for his broad Devonshire accent. He was invited to speak a few lines of dialogue and made such an impact that he was called up to Elstree Studios, for a week's stay, to record his lines. To his great amazement, on entering the studio, he discovered an exact replica of Totnes Guildhall, both the outside and inside, that he knew so well. He was so astonished that he thought he had been whisked back to Devon! He greatly enjoyed his week in London, being treated like a star, staying in a fine hotel, and being given a hefty cheque. However, his elation was marred somewhat a few weeks later when he received a tax demand for his extra earnings!

Other locations which were used in this film include the Seven Stars and other parts of Totnes, Stoke Gabriel, South Brent railway station and Dartmoor. For some reason extras who participated on the moorland shot got double the rate – a little bit more for a bit on the moor perhaps?

The Recluse

There are parts of Devon, in particular to the north of Dartmoor, which are extremely remote. Quiet agricultural backwaters stretch across many miles of countryside dissected by a maze of high hedged lanes. In such a landscape the tide of social and economic change is slow creating, in some cases, some bizarre stories of twentieth century families living the sort of life that would have been far more appropriate to the last century.

Such a situation arose with a family called Luxton of West Chapple Farm near Brushford. The family had farmed the area since the fourteenth century enjoying fluctuating fortunes, some branches of the family achieving great heights whilst others simply bided their time eking out a humble existence from the land. Their insular life style was suddenly made public by a still unsolved triple killing. Brothers Alan and Robert Luxton shared the farm with their domineering sister Frances. One September morning their three bodies were found outside the farmhouse all shot dead. It is presumed that it was a family affair with no outsiders involved.

A film based on these events was made starring Anne Tirard, Maurice Denham and Derek Smith. Although West Chapple Farm was used for the filming, the main characters' names were changed, but the stars met several local people to aquaint themselves with the local accents and something about the nature of the folk they were to depict on the film.

A Riley car was used for some of the shots which featured Maurice Denham and Anne Tirard. The latter was amused and amazed by the lengths to which one cameraman had to go to film them driving along. An enormous sling was set up so that he was driven along with his feet just about on the car and his body was winched out over the road at an alarming angle.

Time was a problem and a strict schedule was adhered to. On the last day of filming an early start was followed by a full days filming which led on until two o'clock the following morning. The reward for their efforts was a BAFTA award for 'best short film'.

Top Secret!

We enjoyed *Top Secret!* and found it very entertaining even though our expectations were not high, having heard that it was an exceedingly dull spy spoof of no real merit. It comes from the same stable as the highly rated spoof air disaster movie *Airplane!*. The only scenes obviously shot in Devon were during the titles at the beginning of the film which, being of some interest to the plot, lasted for several minutes. The scene depicted the all-American beach party with big waves, beautiful girls, surf riding and surf music Beach Boys fashion (the music supposedly coming from the hero, an American rock star who does a tour in Germany and gets mixed up with spies from both sides). The imagination of the director turned Devon's Saunton Sands into 'California' and we see the actors frolicking about in the hot Sunshine State. On closer inspection the sands look rather grey and deserted and, judging by the size of the waves which were the reason for picking this surfing spot, a biting wind is suspected. If you look closely at the girls (if you need an excuse), you may detect goose pimples on their goose pimples! And do look carefully at the hang glider who appears to have soared in from on high … the stack of beer barrels he had been standing on collapsed under him on the first take and he had to jump off them again!

The Shout

This was a very strange film with location filming at Winkleigh and in other parts of North Devon. Its cast included Alan Bates, Susannah York, John Hurt and Tim Curry, all drawn into this 1978 film about a man, who may or may not be mad, who claims that he can kill simply by shouting. The basis of the belief stems from old aborigine magicians, who tend to be in rather short supply in North Devon, who supposedly had such powers.

Water

Despite a lorry load of plastic palm trees and an impressive cast list of Michael Caine, Leonard Rossiter, Billy Connolly, Brenda Vaccaro, Fulton MacKay, Fred (Herman Munster) Gwynne and Martin Tasker, *Water* was a wash out! This film was made at St Lucia in the West Indies (where no plastic palm trees were needed), at Shepperton Studios and in North Devon on the cliffs near Hartland.

The story centres on Cascara, a small tropical island with a poor economy. Things look up when it is suspected that oil might be found. Baxter Thwaites is the Governor, played by Michael Caine, with Brenda Vaccaro as his bored wife. Leonard Rossiter, in his last film before his untimely death, played the uncaring British Government representative, sent to hand the island its unwanted independence. The late Fulton MacKay played an inebriated vicar and Fred Gwynne is a business tycoon, heading the American oil company who accidentally discover an underground reservoir of pure Perrier water. The particular strain of water is deemed to have special properties which would reduce the need for a bowl of fibre every morning and, as such, is seen as a commercially viable product.

The islanders are an odd bunch largely descended from shipwreck victims. Thus, when the Cascaran National Anthem was played, it was accompanied by arm movements depicting first the breast stroke and then the backstroke, commemorating the arrival of the islanders' ancestors. This mild comedy has a few highlights and running jokes, like when the leader of the Revolutionary force (Billy Connolly) refuses to speak and sings out all his political beliefs.

Paul Heiney was involved in this film for the BBC series *In at the Deep End*. Mr Heiney had his hair cut militarily short and joined a band of guerillas planning to blow up the oil/water rig. Despite knowing of his involvement in advance, he isn't easy to spot instantly and therefore should be considered a 'success' at that particular assignment! A local BBC television reporter, Martin Tasker, played a small cameo part as a television reporter. Despite all the ingredients, this film by Dick Clement and Ian La Frenais was not at all convincing. We watched the film on video and gave it four out of ten (we always were generous to a fault!) But then again, it can't be all bad – after all, it was 'Made in Devon'.

THE FINAL CURTAIN

And so to the inevitable final credits where we both would like to thank the entire supporting cast for their various contributions. This has been a difficult book to research and write, one that started as 'just a bit of fun' – and ended as a lot of fun!

Our research has taken us to many places and goodness knows how many television programmes, films or commercials we may have missed whilst we were out working on this book! One thing is for certain, we know there were films 'Made in Devon' that have not been included particularly in the cases where there were also gaps and omissions from the various 'comprehensive' film guides we consulted. Particularly frustrating was the number of films or programmes apparently 'Made in Devon' without local involvement which proved very difficult to follow up. In other cases, lack of substantiating evidence even caused us to begin to doubt what we were told by people who were actually involved in the filming!

A particularly good example of this was in the case of a film we heard was made at Oldway Mansion, Paginton, starring Barry Humphries (not, we believe, as Dame Edna Everage) and another well known Australian, Clive James. It seems that for an entire weekend there were very scantily dressed, nubile females running around the grounds for the sake of the filming. We talked to an extra, normally a taxi driver, who was dressed as a priest for a walk-on part. An elderly spectator was noted to be particularly shocked by the sight of a member of the 'clergy' being involved in

such a risqué venture! Unfortunately the memory of our source failed him as to precise dates and details and we had to give up without even a film title.

Another example is that it was rumoured that Tom Baker, in his role as *Dr Who*, filmed at Holwell Quarry behind Haytor. Our line of enquiries proved fruitless – until this book was already being printed. Then, by accident, we discovered that the film crew and cast had indeed been here and on one occasion had all descended on Webbers shop in Chagford, clearing them out of waterproof garments, not having been warned in advance of the inclement Dartmoor weather!

Therefore this little book should never be treated as an authority on the subject and you are warned that there may be some exaggeration or distortion of what actually happened. After all, most of the stories were passed on by word of mouth and 'theatricals' are always prone to make things more colourful than they might be!

Also, filming in Devon is an ongoing thing and even before the ink was dry in this edition, a wooden mock-up of a lighthouse appeared high on the cliffs at Hartland Quay on Devon's rugged North Coast. This was being built for a three minute sequence in a horror movie and involved a helicopter swirling in over a stormy sea and landing for a dramatic scene. But it is unlikely that anybody who sees the film will identify the location.

So, having read this book and seen the type of story we enjoy passing on, if you have any stories about or details of any television commercials, films or television programmes, made anywhere in South West England, we would love to hear your stories or borrow your pictures. You never know – you may be the star of our next production.

That's all for now folks!

OTHER OBELISK PUBLICATIONS

TALES OF THE UNEXPLAINED IN DEVON by Judy Chard
When you read this book, you will not be shocked or scared out of your wits, nor will you need to pour yourself a stiff drink in order to regain your composure. But you will need to don your thinking cap and ponder over this series of unusual tales, mysterious happenings, and dastardly deeds from various parts of Devon. Judy Chard has leant on her wealth of journalistic experience to intrigue you with a well researched and documented dossier of murders, mysteries, phantom and haunted houses, ley-lines and UFOs. And they say nothing ever happens in Devon...?

THE DEVONAIR BOOK OF HAUNTED HAPPENINGS by Judy Chard
Included in "Haunted Happenings" is a ghost which hitch hikes along the A38, a garage where spanners fly through the air, a full scale military battle only heard in one hotel room, a ghost who steals tea spoons from a pub, a phantom Dartmoor cottage, spirits who smoke cigars, the ghosts of television and radio, various ghostly pets, and many more amazing and mystifying tales about dreams and premonitions which came true. Judy Chard invited listeners to DevonAir Radio to tell their own ghostly happenings and so, with additional contributions from Chips Barber, this is not the usual oft-repeated legends and well-known ghost stories, but a miscellany of inexplicable stories of modern hauntings.

ADVENTURE THROUGH RED DEVON by Raymond B Cattell
This tale is a highly amusing and personal study of the coastline, estuaries, rivers, inland hills, towns and villages of England's most lovely county, as seen in the summers between 1931 and 1935. Despite the passing of more than half a century, the voyages by boat and explorations on foot remain timeless. Raymond Cattell and his friends enjoy a variety of adventures and misadventures encountering gold prospectors and bathing belles at Torquay, an unconscious Newton Abbot, the Desert Island of Dawlish Warren, 'Neptune' near Exmouth, a very superior Sidmouth and lots more.

UNDER SAIL THROUGH SOUTH DEVON AND DARTMOOR by R B Cattell
The windswept, boulder-strewn landscape of Dartmoor and the wild, almost unspoilt coastline of South Devon are two strikingly beautiful areas. In this continuation of adventures begun in "Adventure Through Red Devon", Raymond Cattell encounters nude bathers at Dartington, has a race to the legendary Cranmere Pool, meets a pixie at Princetown, stumbles across a long lost port on The Tamar, is nearly blown up at Berry Head, scorched at Prawle Point and much more. If you have the spirit of adventure and a good sense of fun, you will be thrilled and enthralled by this great Devonshire safari through South Devon and Dartmoor.

THE GREAT WALKS OF DARTMOOR by Terry Bound
This is the first book to include all the recognised long walks which take place on Dartmoor. It includes the Abbots Way, the North/South Crossing, the Lich Way, the Perambulation, the Dartmoor 100, the Mariners Way, the Ten Tors, the OATS walks and the Tom Cobley walk. These walks are sufficiently detailed to enable the fit enthusiast to follow them.

RUNNING IN DEVON by John Legge

The intrepid runners who brave the elements to pound along the city streets or splash their way along muddy Devon lanes are the stars of this little book by John Legge. "Running in Devon" takes us through our paces while looking at the history and background of a great variety of races from large marathons to tiny local events in Devon's villages. Illustrated with many photographs of runners, he recalls road races, relays and cross country events both past and present. It is an informative guide for both the dedicated runner or the 'armchair athlete'.

MEMORIES OF NEWTON ABBOT by Elsie Townsend

Miss Townsend vividly recalls her early life in Newton Abbot between the years 1901 to 1932 and takes us on a nostalgic tour around long forgotten corners of a town that has seen many changes over the years. Celebrations and coronations, festivals and fairs were highlights of everyday life and Elsie tells many stories about the local characters, traders and people who gave the town such a distinctive atmosphere. Illustrated by many old photographs of bygone days, this book is fascinating reading.

ALBERT LABBETT'S CREDITON COLLECTION
by Albert Labbett

Albert Labbett has lived in Crediton all his life and, over the years, has assembled a large collection of photographs of the town. This book contains more than 60 of these black and white photographs showing events and people from the town's past. Celebrations, coronations, festivals, fairs, markets, coaching inns, public houses, elections, transport, traders, trips, sporting teams, industries and local characters all feature prominently in this lovely collection.

AN EXETER BOYHOOD by Frank Retter

Frank reflects on the sort of childhood that many older Exonians will identify with, in an Exeter which was uncompromisingly tough. The story explores the days when Hele's School was opposite Bury Meadow, Exeter's golf course was high above Pennsylvania, electric trams were a revolutionary form of transport and the cattle market was held in Bonhay Road. Illustrated by old and new photographs, and line drawings, it is a fascinating study of life at the turn of the century.

IDE by Bill Rowland

Ide is one of Devon's most beautiful villages. Set in glorious countryside, a few miles from Exeter, its life as a village has generally been quiet and peaceful. Bill Rowland recalls the village life, its characters and buildings, and recounts many lively and amusing stories which both educate and entertain. Quiet country backwater it may well be, but it has never been a dull place!

RAMBLING IN THE PLYMOUTH COUNTRYSIDE
by Dave Woolley & Martin Lister

Covering twelve different walks, this book explores some splendid scenery in and around Plymouth. Well illustrated, it contains many interesting tales from along the coast, up the creeks, and across the commons and downs around Plymouth.

OTHER TITLES BY CHIPS BARBER

AROUND AND ABOUT THE HALDON HILLS
This is a personal study which attempts to portray this hill range in a way which will stimulate the reader to make fuller use of the area. It deals with the obvious and the unusual, the mysterious and the magnificent. You will read of lords and ladies, gypsies and tramps, elephants and swans, the town and villages. The Haldon Hills have much to interest the historian, geologist, rambler, naturalist or simply the curious.

THE LOST CITY OF EXETER
Here is a journey to discover the theatres and cinemas which disappeared long ago, the country streams now well beneath the city streets, the country villages swamped by suburbs and the lost way of life that once existed in Exeter. Full of unusual anecdotes and stories about the real Exeter, this lively book contains many illustrations, including aerial views of the city.

DIARY OF A DARTMOOR WALKER
This is described by the author as 'a libellous log of some fun loving days spent in battle with Dartmoor in all its moods'. It is a lighthearted book which includes many unusual strolls into all areas of Dartmoor and will have enormous appeal to people who already know Dartmoor.

THE TORBAY BOOK
Packed with many strange tales and surprises from Maidencombe, Babbacombe, St Marychurch, Torquay, Cockington, Paignton, Goodrington and Brixham, this book will amaze you with its hundreds of stories – a 'must' for anyone who loves South Devon.

DIARY OF A DEVONSHIRE WALKER
Sequel to Dartmoor Walker, this book contains many Dartmoor walks, but also explores the Haldon Hills, Tamar Valley and South Devon coastline and is perfect for anyone with a sense of fun and adventure who likes walking in Devon, on Dartmoor, the hills or the coast.

THE GREAT LITTLE DARTMOOR BOOK
Beautifully illustrated with line drawings on every page, it features stories of the Moor's folklore and legends, walking and 'Letterboxing', villages and towns, wildlife and tors, pubs and entertainment. This small book is 'big' on text and information and is the perfect "All in One" guide book to Dartmoor.

THE GREAT LITTLE EXETER BOOK
This beautifully illustrated little volume features stories of the City's legends, ghost stories, historical events, important buildings, hotels and pubs, parks and gardens, watercourses, shops, underground passages and famous visitors.

THE DEVONAIR BOOK OF FAMILY WALKS
A leisurely guide to relatively easy jaunts across hill and dale, along coastlines, through woods and forests and all over South and East Devon, suitable for all the family, this well documented little book suggests some wonderful places to explore.

If you have any difficulty in obtaining any of these titles, please contact Obelisk Publications, 2 Church Hill, Pinhoe, Exeter, EX4 9ER. Tel: (0392) 68556.